SAYERS SAY
SAYERS SAY
SAYERS SAY
SAYERS SAY
SAYERS SAY
SAYERS SAY
SAYERS SAY
SAYERS SAY

SAYERS

SCHEMERS
SCHEMERS
SCHEMERS
SCHEMERS
SCHEMERS
SCHEMERS
SCHEMERS
SCHEMERS

SCHEMERS
SCHEMERS
SCHEMERS
SCHEMERS
SCHEMERS
SCHEMERS
SCHEMERS
SCHEMERS

SAINTS
SAINTS
SAINTS
SAINTS
SAINTS
SAINTS
SAINTS
SAINTS

& SAINTS
& SAINTS
& SAINTS
& SAINTS
& SAINTS
& SAINTS
& SAINTS
& SAINTS

LESSONS ON LEADERSHIP

FROM OVERLOOKED MEN

AND WOMEN OF THE BIBLE

SEERS, SAYERS, SCHEMERS & SAINTS
Lessons on Leadership from Overlooked Men and Women of the Bible

Cru Press
100 Lake Hart Drive 2500
Orlando, FL 32832
CruPress.com

Book and Cover Design by Aaron Martin

Edited by Austin Ross

For additional copies:
www.crupress.com
1 (800) 827-2788

ISBN 1-57334-104-7

TOC

Everything was ready. Cookies and drinks filled the tables in the ballroom—the sound system, carefully calibrated, awaited the emcee's opening monologue. Rows of chairs lined all the way to the back of the room. For weeks, invitations had been dispersed and accepted. Only select students received one: a group of scholars attending the university on prestigious academic scholarships. Anita, the originator of this gathering and a brilliant student herself, now stood only a few months removed from that same academic program. A freshly minted staff member with our ministry, Anita desired to influence her peers in the areas of faith and leadership. She designed the program and the ambiance. She personally invited over two hundred people. She heard dozens say that they would attend. She moved about the room, excited and nervous to host this evening that included a lecture I would give on leadership. As the hour approached, Anita and I stood at the door, along with Kathy, our emcee, ready to greet the students as they arrived.

Only they never appeared. The start time for the program came and went. No one walked down the hall. No one approached the door. Finally—fifteen minutes late—one freshman entered the room. Even worse than no one showing up for your event is when only one person comes. Do you cancel or do you press on? Not knowing better, we pressed on as planned. After our emcee enthusiastically greeted us, I mounted the platform. We'd paid a good amount for this platform, specifically so that people in the back of the undoubtedly packed crowd could see the speaker. The one freshman in the audience didn't have any trouble seeing me.

I gave an abbreviated talk on leadership, and afterwards we chatted a bit and sent our guest off with armloads of cookies. Only then did Anita burst into tears. Weeks of praying, planning, hard work, and anticipation resulted in what we all considered a failure. Even with free food we couldn't draw a crowd. We went our separate ways, discouraged and ready to give up on that group of scholarship students.

The next day I looked for Anita at our regular gathering place on campus, planning to commiserate about the previous night—but she was nowhere to be found. I assumed that she needed space and would give her whatever she needed.

But then I learned that after walking to campus that day, Anita headed directly to the dorms where the student scholars lived. She began engaging the same people who stood her up the night before. She invited them to a Bible study she planned on starting. Failure had only strengthened her resolve. Within a few weeks there was a large, dynamic Bible study, led by Anita—and co-hosted by the lone student who attended our event. Many of those student scholars discovered and grew in their faith through that study. Friendships started and lives changed. Anita influenced dozens of the same students who had bailed on her earlier. She proved the power of persistence in the life of a leader. But I grew uneasy.

At the time I was one of the directors of our campus ministry, a new leader just starting in the role. I felt good about leading—nervous at times, but confident that I could handle whatever came my way. I learned to navigate the challenges and problems faced by people in my leadership position. But watching Anita doggedly pursue students created in me an unanticipated anxiety, an apprehension I had not considered. I began to ask myself, "Who was I to lead such a good leader?" It slowly dawned on me that this woman had been entrusted to my care and direction as part of the team I was co-leading, and for the first time I started to understand the quality and value of the people placed under my management. Responsible to lead our team with skill and integrity, I wasn't sure I had what Anita and others like her deserved. Typical days spent speaking in fraternities and planning international mission trips suddenly looked much less challenging. Developing and caring for leaders shook my confidence. Was I up to the task? Could I lead? I felt a serious divide between my team's leadership *needs* and my leadership *skills*. I began to look for resources to pour into that gap. I investigated how to grow in my leadership and how to help others grow with me. This turned into a topic I have continued to pursue ever since that experience in the ballroom over thirty years ago. Reading widely on leadership from dozens and dozens of authors, studying the Bible on the issue, listening to good leaders, and then applying what I've learned, has led to helpful practices and enabled me to help teach others some of those same practices. Leadership, so challenging and so necessary, never goes out of style.

I recently polled sixty ministry leaders with this question: "What are the one or two ideas you would want a young person to grasp as they step into leadership?" This collection of leaders consisted of men and women of diverse ages and various ethnic and national backgrounds. Their answers fell into a few primary categories. Overwhelmingly, veteran leaders underscored the need for young leaders to develop their walk with God. Spiritual leadership involves leading for the Lord and shepherding his flock. Leaders must continually grow toward their master. Next, most mentioned that a leader's role involves making others successful. You serve those you lead; you don't use them for your own ends. As a part of serving, a good leader affirms and encourages those he or she leads. Additionally, these experts wrote about the need to lead with vision and emphasized the importance of leaders who are humble, curious and always learning. Finally, experienced leaders want to see younger leaders lean toward action, who risk and fail and try again.

I wrote this book for three reasons. First, I hope to encourage leaders of all types to step forward. The need exists for good leaders at every level of society. Good people making good decisions are necessary nationally and internationally, and good people making good decisions are needed for state legislatures, local school boards, church committees, business boardrooms, high school and college campuses and the factory floor. As Proverbs says, "a leader of good judgment gives stability while an exploiting leader leaves a trail of waste" (Proverbs 29:5).

My second reason for writing is that I hope to reintroduce you to a few of the fascinating people found throughout the pages of our Bibles. Mini-biographies litter the scriptures, captivating the reader and guiding those open to learn. All waiting just for you! I love reading the Scriptures. I committed to reading the Bible through cover-to-cover annually many years ago. I've just finished my twenty-fifth reading. The Bible never gets old. It's simply unbelievable. Every time I read through it something new and undiscovered unfolds before my eyes. I hope to spread my love of reading and listening to the Bible to you. Along those lines, I want to encourage you to make the Bible your primary life text. We cast about for wisdom and insight everywhere. No shortage of advice exists in our world today, and it's all more easily accessible than ever before. I encourage you to look first to the Bible, not only for lessons in leadership, but to make it your primary life text for every area of life: finances, relationships, family, marriage, work, rest, ethics, politics, environmental issues, immigration, how you treat your neighbors, and what you believe about God. Let the truth found in the Scriptures saturate your thoughts and responses to all of life. Grow into a grounded, biblical follower of Jesus—not just a cultural Christian.

Finally, I hope your reading helps you experience God. I desire that you clearly see God's care and concern for you and as a result you secure a greater trust in the Lord. A unique aspect about the Scriptures are how they are described in Hebrews 4:12: "For the word of God is alive and active. Sharper than any double-edged sword, it penetrates even to dividing soul and spirit, joints and marrow, it judges the thoughts and attitudes of the heart." The Bible on your shelf sits there, waiting to come alive as you open it. Several years ago, my family took a trip to Roatan, Honduras. While there we spent an afternoon snorkeling in perhaps the most beautiful coral reef in the world. From the beach, the reef remained out of site, hidden under the serene blue waters of the Caribbean. Our guide loaded us onto his boat for a five minute ride into the bay, then dropped us into the water. Once submerged, a new world opened before our eyes. We were swimming atop a massive underwater trench, lined with coral and filled with a limitless array of living creatures. The brilliant colors of fish and coral danced with the sunlight to create an otherworldly scene. After swimming along the surface for a few minutes, we dove deeper. We noticed caves in the coral, fins flashing in their depths. Far below us, scuba divers emerged from mysterious fissures. Everywhere you looked you saw life, and the deeper we plunged the more we noticed. That is the way the Bible works in our lives: Within its pages you find life in abundance, and the deeper you dive the more you will discover.

In the following pages you will find stories of leaders. Good leaders and lousy leaders, brave leaders and cowards. Human leaders. Real people. You'll find leaders God used and others from whom he stepped away. Throughout you will discover principles demonstrated by their leadership. My hope is that these stories help you lead better and influence more people for the kingdom of God. I hope the lives described in these pages pull you back to the scriptures for yourself, that you will be intrigued enough to open your Bible and read more. I hope that you apply what you read, for the good of yourself and the good of those around you. Finally, I hope that you'll experience more of the Lord. Not just in an academic sense, but in a visceral, down in the gut sense of knowing that God is with you and for you as you lead.

CHAPTER ONE

PHARAOH'S DAUGHTER

EXODUS 1 & 2

The young mother, frantic to conceal her infant son who was under a death sentence, knew her time was running out. In desperation she attempted a wild scheme. She gently placed her son in a waterproof basket and set it afloat near the royal women bathing in the river, hoping both in God and in the latent maternal instinct of a sheltered princess. The boy drifted in the reeds and was soon discovered safe and sound by the daughter of the king.

We need to take a quick look at the history of Israelites in Egypt in order to really understand what comes next. The descendants of Israel lived, just as they had for the past 400 years, in Egypt—driven there by the great famine during the time of Joseph. It was in Egypt that they multiplied into a large nation. So large, in fact, that Pharaoh, the king of the Egyptians, started to get nervous. "The Swayer of the Universe," as he was sometimes called, worried that the Hebrews might join his enemies in a future invasion, despite 400 years of good citizenship. So, like any respectable despot, Pharaoh enslaved the Hebrews, forcing them to labor on the great cities he was building to honor himself. The Egyptians ruthlessly exploited the Hebrews. Not confident that he could work the Hebrews to death, Pharaoh embarked on a fresh genocidal policy, decreeing that all the newborn boys of the Hebrews were to be thrown into the Nile and drowned. Naturally, the Hebrews did all they could to protect their babies.

Which brings us to a little boy named Moses. Born during this brutal time, his distraught yet resourceful mother hid him as long as she could before embarking on her plan. The waters of the Nile guided the basket to the hands of Bithiah, Pharaoh's daughter, showing that God is nothing if not ironic. Bithiah ordered her servants to pull Moses from the river and she immediately recognized him as Hebrew.

The next decision she made was critical. The policy was to kill all the Hebrew baby boys, but Bithiah took pity and rescued Moses. This defied the edict of her own father, and she could have been killed for her disregard of Pharaoh's orders. Nevertheless, Bithiah took Moses as her son and raised him in the royal house of Egypt. This act of mercy—also an act of civil disobedience—saved the rescuer of Israel.

A leader is nothing without mercy. It's one thing to stride forward in victory, to make the impossible happen or to finally secure the job that sets you up for life. It's another issue altogether to advance by stepping on the backs of others. To live your life, to enjoy the fruits of success and the wonders offered to you, but to ignore the baby in the bulrushes misses the point of leadership. The helpless and vulnerable, the person in need of mercy, *is the point*. Jesus tells us, "blessed are the merciful, for they will be shown mercy" (Matthew 5:7). Truly, aren't we all babies floating helplessly along, waiting for a savior to pull us from the water and give us life? Blessed was Bithiah, the daughter of a wicked king. Her mercy still instructs today and a leader will do well to emulate her example.

CHAPTER TWO

EXODUS 32

The Israelites were stranded in the wilderness at the foot of a smoking, fiery mountain. They were tired of waiting on Moses to come back from that mountain, so they decided to take matters into their own hands. Before Moses vanished into the mist, he left his brother and spokesperson, Aaron, in charge, so the people naturally turned to him for leadership and direction. The pressure on Aaron to do something must have been enormous. Without his brother by his side, Aaron struggled to stay faithful to God. When the leaders of Israel demanded a new set of gods, he did not object, but rather complied enthusiastically.

Aaron told the Israelites to bring him all their gold, which he then melted down and fashioned an idol—specifically a golden calf—for the nation to worship. An important note here is that bulls had endured as an important object of worship in ancient Egypt, so Aaron was molding something familiar for the people. What we don't know is his motivation for doing this. He may have felt that the people needed a physical representation of God, or he may have felt that God had abandoned Israel. He may have acted simply out of fear of the mob. Regardless, Aaron ultimately led the nation *away* from God as he raised the golden calf on a pedestal, leading the cheers of "these are your gods, O Israel, who brought you up out of the land of Egypt!" The people rejoiced. They worshipped the calf and sacrificed to it. It is remarkable that the same people who walked on dry ground while the Red Sea had been split in half on either side of them turned whole-heartedly to this calf. This community, who experienced wonders saints only dream of, who felt the heat from the pillar of fire on their faces, now turned aside to a calf, made of their own jewelry, in wonder. After Moses disappeared, they abandoned the Lord and turned to a safer god, a more manageable deity.

What is your golden calf? Where do you put your faith when you forget the God of heaven? It's hard to be patient, to trust in the Lord, to wait. It's also hard to serve a God that we cannot see. We so desire a tangible, hold-in-your-hands and see-with-your-own-eyes god. We compromise too easily; we sell ourselves at a bargain price. Aaron gave in to the cries of the people so quickly; we don't observe a bit of hesitation or argumentation on his part. Moses left the nation of Israel in slack hands and Aaron crumbled as soon as opposition arose. Aaron failed as a leader.

In many ways, a leader must be flexible and seek to compromise for the good of the cause and the good of others. However, in the foundational truths, of which there are only a few, a leader must be steadfast. Too quickly did Aaron abandon the truths and the ways of the Lord. Too quickly did Aaron leave the unseen to grab for the visible and the tangible. A calf in the hand felt safer than a rumbling mountain, despite all that Aaron has already seen and experienced. Sometimes even the miraculous cannot overcome the dark timidity of our hearts.

As a leader, where are you tempted to turn from the God of the mountain to a calf of gold? What might you be tempted to give up in order to appease the crowd? Where might you be choosing expediency rather than truth? A leader must prepare herself for a more difficult path. The crowd will ask for ease, for immediate answers and simple compromises. The leader's job is to take her people to the mountain, to help communities find hope in the living God. It will always feel easier to surrender, like Aaron did, and give people what they want. But it will not be better or safer or, in the end, kinder. Only in Yahweh, the God of the Mountain, can hope be found. Aaron learned the hard way that a first-class calf is a poor substitute for the living God. He chose poorly. Like Aaron, we all get to choose. Select either the unpredictable, untamed, immortal, omnipotent God of the blazing mountaintop, who does not answer to any of us, or take the flavorless safety of a metal cow you carry in your pocket. As a leader, what is your choice? As a leader, where is your hope?

CHAPTER THREE

CALEB

NUMBERS 13 & 14
JOSHUA 14 & 15
JUDGES 3

The mob ruled the day. No amount of reason or vision could sway their fears, nor could any fervent pleas from the nation's leaders. A whisper campaign eroded any support that may have remained after the arrival of the spies. This timid multitude, desperate to escape, imagined visions of monsters preparing to grind them to dust. When the throng, now numbering tens of thousands, crested at the peak of its anger, only four men opposed their calls to return to enslavement in Egypt. Moses, Aaron and Joshua tore their clothes in a sign of grief at the loss of the people's courage. The crowd stood unmoved. A fourth man, one of the spies who was with Joshua, then ripped his coat and gave this speech: "The land we passed through and explored is exceedingly good. If the Lord is pleased with us, He will lead us into that land, a land flowing with milk and honey, and will give it to us. Only do not rebel against the Lord. And do not be afraid of the people of the land, because we will swallow them up. Their protection is gone, but the Lord is with us. Do not be afraid of them." Caleb, convinced of the Lord's goodness towards Israel, pleaded for sanity, for the people to remember the Lord's leading of their nation. The mob's response? Swift talk of stoning all four leaders. Imagine pelting Moses with rocks, the man who led the nation out of Egypt, though the sea on dry ground and across a desert now flowing with water. How quickly fear generates forgetfulness and leads to panic. The talk of stoning didn't last any longer than it took to reach down and pick up a rock. God intervened, blasted the scene with his glory and threatened to destroy them all. After a conversation with Moses, the Lord relented, but not without declaring the punishment the nation would face for rejecting the land promised to them.

Caleb first appears to readers of scripture at this watershed moment in the history of Israel. Moses led the people out of Egypt, and the vast horde that made up the nation of Israel camped at the edge of the Promised Land. Finally, after hundreds of years of waiting and praying and hoping, their dreams existed as a reality only a few steps away. In order to gain much needed intelligence, Moses chose a team of spies—undercover agents, really—to send into this new land. Trailblazers from each tribe, handpicked for this dangerous assignment, started the expedition with high hopes, Caleb included. These hopes soon paled. Ten of the twelve spies perceived the inhabitants of the land as giants with overwhelming strength. In their sight, the men of Israel cowered like grasshoppers before these behemoths who would devour their nation. Only two of the spies, Caleb and Joshua (the future successor of Moses) understood the situation differently. Facing a panicked crowd with death on its mind, Caleb and Joshua issued a hopeful report, trying to stem the tide of alarm. All to no avail. Fear ruled the day. The mob turned away from their promised land and away from the Lord who led them there.

One of the first lessons a leader needs to understand is that not everyone will like you or your leadership. Some will oppose you to your face and one or two might threaten you like they did with Caleb. Others may undermine your agenda, either by passive indifference or active rebellion, or they may call your methodology into question. Just know that conflict and adversity will come your way. Adversity follows leaders like night follows day. Don't act surprised when it shows up. Step into adversity and lead.

One of the depressing aspects of leadership and life in general is that we often deal with the consequences of other people's poor decisions. Caleb stepped into such a situation. Angered at the people's response to the bad report from the spies, the Lord sent a plague to kill the ten cowardly spies and then banished the entire nation of Israel to the desert for forty years. Doomed to wander until an entire generation died off, the people turned away from their hoped-for future. No milk or honey, flowing or otherwise. Totally depressing. Where did this leave Caleb, the spy who did exactly the right thing? Caleb represented the Lord wholeheartedly, passionately, even vigorously, all at the risk of his own life. Where did he go? Out into the desert with everyone else. Caleb swallowed a bitter pill. Caleb followed God fully yet he still got the same punishing news - back away from the Promised Land.

Sometimes as a leader you get the shaft. Bad things happen to good leaders. Caleb spent forty years wandering

around the desert, living every single day around the people
who rejected his leadership. He moved the tents with them,
he herded the livestock with them, he gathered manna with
them and he listened to them bitch and moan about their
sore feet and their desert wanderings. Not a wonderful life.
On top of that, Caleb attended lots and lots of funerals.
Everyone his age, friends and family members, parents,
brothers, sisters, cousins and all those of that generation,
died while in the wilderness.

How did Caleb respond? He remained hopeful and persevered. Despite forty years in a desert surrounded by
cowards, Caleb kept his faith in the Lord. Here's a truth
I've seen again and again, one I didn't understand when
I was younger: *Time is the most difficult test most leaders
face.* Time tests your character. It checks the depth of your
faith. It saps your energy and strength. It takes your health.
Time allows the world's systems to erode your belief in the
redeemer God. Time tires you out, and when you're tired it's
easy to quit. You cannot escape the tests of time; you can
only prepare to meet them.

Caleb did not quit. The Lord promised Caleb that he would
enter the Promised Land. Only Caleb and Joshua, two of
an entire generation, received that promise. Caleb clung
to his promise from God; it carried him. God's promises,
as discovered in scripture, carry leaders to this day. God's
word is solid ground for a leader. Jesus described it as a rock
and taught us that a wise person builds their house upon it.
Wise leaders continue to build in such a way today. For forty
years, Caleb stood strong. Let that soak in for a minute. Our
world directs us in the opposite direction: Get out of a bad
situation as fast as you can, nothing lasts for forty years.
Most newlywed couples, after pledging their faithfulness

for a lifetime, don't make it to forty years. Jobs don't last forty years, few live in the same house for forty years. Your new car won't last forty years. Think about Caleb in light of our world. Forty years leaves no room for shortcuts. Caleb persevered.

Caleb passed the test of time and forty years later he found himself at the border of this wonderful land of promise. At this point in his life, Caleb was eighty-five years old and he was not about waiting. Caleb stomped over to Joshua's tent, thumped his chest and declared that he was as strong as ever was and ready for war. "Give me that mountain," he demanded of Joshua. If the Lord was in it, Caleb would take the hill country or die trying. Joshua blessed Caleb, and with a grin on his face for his oldest friend, sent Caleb out to take the land.

I desperately hope that at age eighty-five I have the energy to jump into a new challenge. When opportunities arise, leaders act, even when action involves risk. Caleb could have been killed in that endeavor. He did not just send people into a dangerous place, he led them there. Sometimes it's tempting for a leader to rest, to let a good opportunity pass by. Not so with Caleb. He did not want to miss out on God's promise. The test of opportunity arises for successful leaders. Is what I have and what I've done worth risking again for a new and untried opportunity? Learn bravado from Caleb and step from the sidelines, because if you're still breathing, God still has a place for you in the game.

Caleb didn't go it alone. He entered the land with his tribe, his people. In the midst of the battles, Caleb made an interesting proposal. He offered his daughter in marriage to the man who would capture a particular city. Unorthodox, to say the least. Othniel, Caleb's nephew, stepped forward, seized the city and was awarded with Caleb's daughter as his prize. Caleb, himself advanced in age, knew that his tribe required a fresh generation of leaders. He also knew that his daughter needed a good husband, one who could handle life in this chaotic period of conquest and fighting. Caleb set out to accomplish both. Caleb entrusted a young leader with capturing a city. We gain a glimpse at his focus on developing others and we see his desire to help the next generation prosper. A good leader always thinks about who is coming next and how to develop those greener in their leadership journey. Othniel could have blown his chance to take the city. Caleb took a risk on a young leader and it paid off. Leaders pass down authority. Leaders must also learn to pass down control. Control is insidious in the life of a leader. Too much control on the part of a leader stifles initiative in others and drives healthy young leaders away. Let go, flex, and give away control. Trust the Lord to provide others to lead. Like Caleb, entice young leaders to charge forward. A wise, older leader helps younger leaders prosper. Always look to develop the next generation.

Do you realize that the Christian faith is only one generation away from going defunct? Every generation must believe afresh and without leaders, our next generation is at the mercy of the world's influences and forces. This is where Israel found itself several years after finally entering the land. Caleb and Joshua were dead. The entire group of people who led the nation into the promised land passed into glory. Their children took charge and swiftly made a mess of things. The situation got so bad that the Lord, in a disciplinary move, allowed them to be conquered and oppressed by their surrounding enemies. It's amazing how quickly this change occurred. From one generation to the next, in a time

span of roughly forty years, the conquerors became the conquered. To reject the Lord carries consequences, even if you
are of a chosen people. It's tempting to judge from our perch
so many years later, but in our hearts we know that we're the
same.

As you read in the book of Judges you find that the Lord
heard the cries of the anguished, oppressed Israelites as they
called to him. In response, the Lord provided a deliverer.
Astonishingly, back onto the stage stepped Othniel, Caleb's
nephew and son-in-law. Othniel went to war and defeated
the oppressors, doubtlessly applying lessons first learned
from capturing that city so many years before. Thanks to
Othniel's victory, the land and the people enjoyed forty
years of rest. Or, we might say that thanks to Caleb, Othniel
developed into the type of leader God could use. Othniel
grew up in the desert, hearing stories from his uncle Caleb,
the spy. Othniel's father died in the wilderness leaving Caleb
to take an even larger role in Othniel's life. Caleb offered his
daughter to anyone who took that city and Othniel leapt at
that chance, not just to gain the bride-to-be, but to make
good in the eyes of Caleb. Notice the rhythms of their lives.
Like Caleb, Othniel risked his life to take the land. Like
Caleb, Othniel persevered forty years in the midst of a dis-
believing generation. Like Caleb, Othniel seized an opportunity and laid everything he had on the line. Like Caleb,
Othniel received the Lord's reward due to his faithfulness.
Caleb's life, his work and his faith found ultimate fulfillment
not in the hill country he so desired, but in the life, work and
faith of his nephew, Othniel.

In the economy of the Lord, where small investments yield
large dividends, investing in people produces the greatest
returns. Invest in others. Develop the next generation. Teach

them the ways of the Lord. Those are the lessons of Caleb. Caleb's faith won him a mountain. Othniel's faith saved a nation. Whose faith are you influencing today?

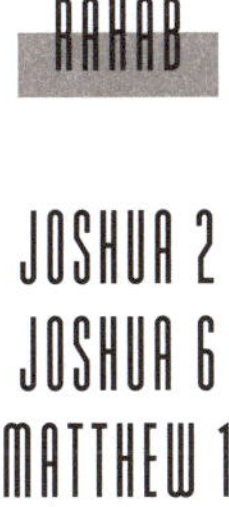

CHAPTER FOUR

RAHAB

JOSHUA 2
JOSHUA 6
MATTHEW 1

Men came every evening for Rahab. Her profession paid well and as a result her family survived from one day to the next. In spite of seemingly endless nights of foul-smelling men, lecherous advances and unspeakable acts, this prostitute greeted the sunrise with a single thought: "Something, or someone, must exist beyond this hell I'm living." Then salvation appeared on the horizon. Of all the people in Jericho, only a whore saw God in the midst of the invading forces of Israel.

Rahab was a prostitute and a hero. She sold her body to men hungering for sex, and she supported her family by doing so. The word "complicated" only *begins* to explain Rahab's life. Over and over again, you'll discover that the Bible does not sugarcoat reality. Gritty, tenacious and genuine, the Bible portrays the people of God as they truly were.

Rahab lived in Jericho while the nation of Israel, led by Joshua, moved to enter and conquer their promised land. In front of Israel raged the flooded Jordan River—and beyond that, the walled city of Jericho. Joshua, a prudent military leader and sound strategist, needed intelligence on the defenses of Jericho. He sent two spies to investigate. After reconnoitering the city, they took shelter in Rahab's house. Why would the spies choose a bordello? Where else in a foreign city could two strangers go that wouldn't arouse much suspicion? Neighbors saw a couple of guys from out of town just looking for a good time. However, the King of Jericho soon discovered the ruse and sent for the men. Rahab improvised quickly. She hid the spies on the roof and sent the searchers off in the wrong direction.

Why would Rahab risk her life and those of her family in order to protect spies from a nation bent on conquest? Rahab told the spies that she was overwhelmed by the works that the God of Israel has done. "For the Lord your God is God in heaven above and on the earth below." The reputation of the God of Israel preceded the nation's arrival. Rahab never imagined such a God. When confronted with the acts of Jehovah she exchanged her old gods for the new. Rahab recognized her hope. She chose to serve the God of Israel. I wonder if Rahab's openness to this new God resulted in part from her life in Jericho? A prostitute, an outcast, desperate. God brings hope to the desperate. Her fellow citizens looked to the sky filled with the choking dust of an invading army and experienced a sense of dread, while Rahab felt a lift in her heart.

Rahab helped the spies escape the city and return to

Joshua in order to make their full report. But not before working a deal. She saved the spies and later they protected her and her family. When the city was conquered and the population put to the sword, the spies rescued and shielded Rahab and her family.

What do we learn from Rahab? What do the actions of an ancient prostitute demonstrate to us about leadership? In Rahab we see a woman enthralled by the power of God. She not only observed how God worked amongst Israel, but she deliberated and decided to go all in. Rahab realized that the God of Israel is a liberator, not an oppressor, and Rahab craved liberation. As in the case of enslaved sex workers today, Rahab needed rescuing. Those two spies came in the name of the True Rescuer.

Rahab thought on her feet. She was adaptable and exceptionally brave. What would have happened if the king of Jericho had discovered her lie? Undoubtedly, it would have cost Rahab and her family their lives. No king is going to spare the life of a mere prostitute. But no matter, whether from faith or desperation or a dramatic combination of both, Rahab made her decision to help the spies and to welcome the armies of Israel into the city of Jericho.

Perhaps the greatest lesson we learn from Rahab's story is the worth we must place on the people around us. Every life is valuable, every individual important. We do not know who God might use to accomplish his purposes. It might be a king or it might be a prostitute. God regards all people as valuable, regardless of their station in life. Similarly, God can use anyone to lead, influence and accomplish his purposes—even the least likely of us.

Rahab risked her life and the lives of her family in order to embrace a God she only saw in the distance. She made her choice by faith, trusting in God and the good will of Israel's spies. Rahab exemplifies a discerning leader, a leader who calculates, a leader able to read conditions and make decisions. She trusts her judgment and moves forward with boldness and conviction.

In the end, how did things work out for Rahab? In the first chapter of Matthew, there's a list of the genealogy of Jesus— and on this list are dozens of men, but only four women. One of those women is a prostitute named Rahab. Matthew tells us that Rahab married Salmon, one of the two spies she hid on her rooftop, and was the mother of Boaz, the great-great-grandmother of King David and a direct ancestor of Jesus. The public exposure of a harlot in the family tree tends to shame distinguished families. But the author of Matthew found it a significant point of pride to reveal that Rahab's blood, the blood of a prostitute and a hero, flowed through the veins of Jesus.

CHAPTER FIVE

JUDGES 4

We all have bad days. But some days are the worst. Sisera experienced one of these days, starting with an overwhelming defeat of his army and ending with a tent peg in his head—but we'll get to that soon enough. Sisera arrived as one of many challenges Israel faced during the era of the Judges, one that felt more like the Wild West than the Middle East. The key phrase from the book of Judges that describes the atmosphere of the day was that "everyone did what was right in their own eyes." No king reigned in Israel. No central authority enforced the laws and defended the borders. The land suffered multiple invasions, years of enemy control and general lawlessness. People grew hard in mind and spirit. In between foreign occupations, a series of judges ruled Israel. The fourth of these judges was Deborah.

Deborah served as the only female judge in this long line of leaders. She is also described as a prophet, as the Lord spoke through her. We don't know how she came into this role, but Deborah led wisely and the people trusted her. At one point, the Lord spoke to her concerning Israel's enemy, the Canaanites. The Lord heard the prayers of the people and moved to free them from this threat. In order to do so, Deborah summoned Barak, another leader in Israel, to lead an army against the unvanquished general Sisera and the Canaanites. Barak recruited 10,000 men for the upcoming battle and shrewdly asked Deborah to accompany the army, again underscoring the value the people placed in her leadership. The armies clashed and Israel routed the Canaanites, partly due to a fortuitous downpour that negated the advantage of Sisera's 900 iron chariots by making it too muddy to maneuver. Barak's army killed every last one of Sisera's troops.

Except they did not catch Sisera. He fled on foot and found refuge with a woman named Jael. She invited the desperate general into her tent, gave him a nourishing cup of fresh milk and agreed to stand guard over him. Sisera, exhausted and with a belly full of milk, fell into a deep sleep. Bad time for a nap. As he snored, Jael realized her opportunity. She took a long tent peg and drove it through Sisera's temple. Jael, a stone cold killer, emerged as a hero of the realm. Hospitable and ruthless.

What do we take from these strange events? First, when it comes to leadership, gender or societal standing does not bind the Lord. God choose Deborah to lead Israel in times of both peace and war. The people of Israel came to her to have their disputes decided. They lived by her decisions. People want someone who is fair and impartial when looking to settle their legal issues. Deborah served the nation well and became that trusted leader that blesses everyone they lead.

Second, it never hurts to be good with a hammer. Jael made a snap decision. What moved her to end the life of

Sisera as he lay passed out on her floor? Did the Lord whisper into her ear? Did the leadership of Deborah provide a positive example of what a woman could accomplish? Or was she simply moved by revenge against the oppressor at her feet? Regardless, she acted without hesitation and a nation gained its freedom.

Third, be careful whose tent you nap in. If you use people to further your agenda without regard to their needs, don't expect them to come to your aid when you are down. Don't linger in the presence of people you've treated poorly. You may not deserve a tent peg to the head, but you will eventually reap what you've sown in your fields of leadership.

The combined actions of Deborah and Jael resulted in four decades of quiet and rest for the nation. Years of fairness and integrity built Deborah's reputation as a leader. Barak followed her plan without question because she exemplified trust. Alongside them both, Jael pitched her tent in the right place at the right time, a woman unafraid and ready to act. To drive the point home (bad pun), her reputation surfaced from a quick decision leading to a grisly act. Two women, two leaders, acted bravely and blessed the lives of thousands. Whether a reputation is built over time or in an instant, good leaders act when opportunities appear.

SAMSON AND THE PHILISTINES

JUDGES 16

Around 1100 BC the famed colossus Samson roamed the earth. Throughout his life, Samson used his prodigious strength to confound and confuse and defeat the Philistines, Israel's persecutors and next-door neighbors. At one point, he killed 1,000 Philistine soldiers with the jawbone of a donkey in a single encounter. Seriously. "Heaps upon heaps," the King James Version of the Bible says. Obviously, Samson had something going on in the hand-to-hand combat realm. He was made for mixed martial arts.

Although Samson laid out mounds of enemies with that jawbone, he crumbled before women. He matched his stunning success in personal combat with equally spectacular failures in his relationships. No matter what the situation, Samson went big. Which brings us to the other individual forever paired with Samson—Delilah, his scheming lover. Delilah was a Philistine and a spy. Under her constant nagging, Samson eventually broke down, told her the secret of his strength and fell asleep on her lap. Moments later, after a fresh haircut, the Lord left Samson and his enemies arrived. Samson woke up bald and beaten and weak—and worst of all, without the Lord. The Philistines took their long desired revenge. They gouged out his eyes and put him in prison. There they forced Samson to turn a huge wheel to grind their grain, like the big, dumb ox he proved himself to be. What an ignoble end to Samson's story as the leader of Israel.

Only that was not the end. We are told that his hair began to grow back and with it, his strength. Later, the Philistines threw a raging party and brought Samson out in front of the crowd. What a perfect night to gloat over Samson's broken body, to celebrate their victory over Israel, and to praise their magnificent god, Dagon. A servant led Samson, now with scars for eyes, out to the auditorium and stood him in the middle of their great temple.

Here we must pause to point out the leadership lessons we learn from the life of Samson. Most obviously, be careful who you trust. Not every friend is good for you. Sometimes we meet a person like Delilah who does not have our best interests at heart, even though they seem like a wonderful person and say all the right things. Samson should have known better, but he preferred Delilah—until his eyes were gouged out. Don't let this happen to you. The next lesson, as we will soon see, is no less important. Take full advantage of second chances. Even if something does not work out the first time, the Lord frequently brings about another opportunity to make things right. Not always, but often. When that happens to you, jump in and do what you couldn't do the first time. Exploit the possibility. Redeem yourself. Chances are strong that the opportunity won't reappear for a third time.

Samson redeemed himself. Placing his hands on the two load-bearing pillars of the temple, he cried out to the Lord for one last burst of strength. The Lord granted Samson his prayer. Samson shifted the pillars, destroying the temple and killing everyone inside. Which brings us to the final leadership lesson from Samson's life, this one being the ultimate lesson experienced by those Philistines in Dagon's temple—*paybacks are hell.*

RUTH 1-4

She was an outsider and an immigrant—the wrong ethnicity, wrong gender, wrong social class. Yet this woman is, like Rahab, mentioned in the genealogy of Jesus in the first chapter of Matthew. How did a woman with so much going against her find redemption? What is so compelling about her life and her character that the gospel writer wanted to make sure that people for all time know that Jesus descended from her stock? What can we learn from her example?

The story of Ruth remains both timeless and wonderful. A Jewish family immigrated to the neighboring country of Moab due to a terrible famine in their homeland, Judah. They settled down and their two sons married local girls: Orpah and Ruth. Unfortunately, tragedy shadowed this family as the father and then his two sons died quickly in succession. Naomi, the wife and mother of the boys, was left alone with her two daughters-in-law. Naomi faced a precarious situation. She was an immigrant in a foreign land with no job or income. Her only connections in Moab were Orpah and Ruth, who were native and of the age to remarry and build new families with new husbands and new in-laws, leaving no room for Naomi. Naomi needed to return to Judah, to her homeland and her family, where she could at least survive. In her kindness, Naomi encouraged Ruth and Orpah to stay in Moab and create a new life for themselves. Orpah chose just that, but Ruth could not bear to part with Naomi. Ruth clung to Naomi and cried out the line shared at so many wedding ceremonies ever since: "Where you will go I will go and where you will stay I will stay. Your people will be my people and your God my God." Naomi, in her vast grief at the loss of her husband, her sons, her home and her dreams, started the long walk back to Bethlehem with one loyal and faithful friend, Ruth.

Nothing rivals the value of a loyal friend. We are not told the reason for Ruth's devotion to her mother-in-law, but something deep inside her just would not let Naomi go alone. Ruth and Naomi trekked all the way back to Judah and reversed roles; Ruth was now the immigrant and Naomi the native. Unsurprisingly, Ruth's presence and loyalty soon drew attention.

The two widows had to find a way to feed themselves. Gleaning behind the harvesters looked like a good option, so Ruth began to pick the grain that the men missed along the way. This was common practice in that era, but dangerous to be an unprotected woman, especially a foreign woman, in the fields alone. When Ruth suggested the practice, Naomi directed her to glean in the fields of her close relative, a man named Boaz. Here, the tragic story takes a beautiful turn. Boaz noticed Ruth and began to show her favor, protecting and providing for her. He clearly kept his eyes on her and their relationship blossomed into marriage. If there is a "happily-ever-after" story in the Bible, this is it.

Ruth displayed resilience and fortitude when faced with the tragic circumstances of her husband's death. Ruth honored her mother-in-law and cared for her in the midst of her own grief. Ruth chose to go with Naomi into an unknown future. Then living in Judah as a foreigner, Ruth quickly discerned that survival depended on her ability to get food by gleaning behind the harvesters. Between Naomi's direction and her hard work and ingenuity, Ruth endeared herself to Boaz, her future husband. The Lord blessed their union with a child, whom they named Obed, which means "worshipper." Obed became the grandfather of King David, who in turn worshipped God with his whole heart.

Why did the Apostle Matthew highlight Ruth in his lineage of Jesus found in Matthew? I believe that it was important to remind us that the bloodline of Jesus is not authoritative or special due to a purity of ethnicity or pedigree, but it is distinctive due to the qualities of his ancestors, including an immigrant woman named Ruth. Ruth demonstrated loyalty, adaptability, quick thinking and an ability to take advantage of an opportunity. We learn a great deal from Ruth. Pray for friends like her and hire people with these qualities. Cultivate these attributes as a leader. Hang onto people like Ruth, who demonstrated these abilities in abundance and who passed on these traits to a long line of future kings, including the king of kings.

1 SAMUEL 14

Jonathan was itching for a fight. He was bored. Muzzled by a passive king, Jonathan sat in his tent and moped. It did not help that that timid king happened to be Jonathan's father, Saul. The nation of Israel existed in a constant state of conflict with their enemies, the Philistines. At this stage in that strife, the Philistines possessed the stronger army and thus the upper hand. To say that the army of Israel lacked basic equipment grossly understated their problem as only Jonathan and Saul even owned a sword and a spear. The rest of the army prepared to fight with farm implements, like pitchforks and axes and sharpened sticks. As you can imagine, the king and his advisors deliberately waited for the right time to engage with the more experienced and better-equipped Philistines. Jonathan, however, could wait no longer. While others measured the enemy and perceived an unbeatable force, Jonathan watched and saw a challenge. Jonathan had to act. Good or bad, Jonathan decided to make something happen. His plan involved confronting the

Philistines, then fighting them wherever that may be and at whatever advantage the Philistines may choose. Jonathan recruited only one other person to go with him—his armor-bearer. Game for the adventure, this young companion replied, "Go ahead; I am with you heart and soul." If you're going to do something crazy, it's always nice of have a sidekick along, even if it's just to post the video on social media.

Let's review Jonathan's plan: If the Philistines told him and his buddy to "wait where you are," then they would wait and deal with what came to them. If the Philistines said, "Come on up," then they would climb up the cliff. Either way, the plan involved fighting the Philistines.

The Philistines chose the latter and watched as Jonathan and his servant scrambled up the rocks to get to them. Big mistake. After getting to the top, Jonathan went to work. No match for the enraged Hebrew, the Philistines fell wounded and bleeding before the sword of Jonathan. Any worthy assistant cleans up after the boss, and so the armor-bearer followed behind and dispatched each man with a sword thrust. Jonathan and his friend killed about twenty Philistine warriors in the space of about half a football field. Bodies and blood everywhere, carnage on the cliff top. This skirmish sparked a general rout. The entire Philistine army panicked. Jonathan's bravery finally moved even his father and Saul led the army of Israel into action. A great victory followed. All predicated on the aggressive action of Jonathan, the warrior prince.

Sometimes a leader goes looking for a fight. To use more modern, and perhaps less violent, language, Jonathan exhibited the behavior of a change agent, someone no longer satisfied with the status quo, a person who brings useful and adaptable transformation. Compelled to do something—anything—even if dangerous, Jonathan confronted his problems, all of whom happened to have Philistine names and swords. Jonathan deemed the status of the army and the nation of Israel as unacceptable and for him that meant something must be done.

How about you? Where are you discontented? Where do you desire to bring change? What frustrates you about the world around you? Where might the Lord press a sense of profound dissatisfaction into your psyche? If nothing comes to mind, are you brave enough to pray and ask the Lord for a piece of his profound dissatisfaction? Plenty of things in this world need changing—will you help drive that change?

Contrast Jonathan's actions with the hesitancy of his father, Saul. While king, Saul possessed great resources and power. Nevertheless, his fear kept him in the camp, perpetually waiting for just the right time to move. Remember how Goliath confronted the army of Israel for forty days before David stepped up to slay the giant? Different story, same king, same faintheartedness. Saul made friends with passivity and never broke off the relationship. Passivity is poison in the life of a leader. Patience serves a leader, but when patience turns into a crust for an underlying heart of fear, everyone suffers. A wise leader discerns the difference. A leader leans into fear. One truth I've learned over many years is that action conquers fear. Stand, walk, or run, just do something. Find a buddy and climb a cliff. See what needs to change around you and see how Lord shows up and joins you.

DAVID & GOLIATH

1 SAMUEL 17

The story of David and Goliath doesn't mean what you think it does. We tend to think of it as a story where the underdog takes on and defeats a much stronger and better-experienced opponent. We use this metaphor all the time in sports—think of a movie like *Miracle*, which tells the real-life story of when the 1980 U.S. Olympic hockey team, made up of college players, defeated the highly favored Soviet team. Every year some upset victory somewhere in the world earns the "David Defeats Goliath" headline. We love this kind of story and we love to root for the underdog. In this case however, David was no underdog.

On the surface, the account found in 1 Samuel 17 follows this script. Goliath is a legitimate giant, highly experienced in the art of war and hand-to-hand combat. David, on the other hand, stood to about Goliath's navel and had never fought in a battle. David carried zero experience in combat as he walked to the skirmish line. David, however, knew how to kill. If you read this chapter in 1 Samuel carefully, you'll discover David's fighting pedigree. Although new to fighting Philistines, David previously fought and killed lions and bears while defending his family's sheep. Consider for a moment the astounding assertion made in this passage—don't just skim over what David is saying. David, as a young shepherd, claimed to have killed at least one lion and one bear, using a sling and his bare hands. David was just a teenager, but he was unlike any teenager I've ever met.

David's experience tending sheep and protecting them from predators prepared him marvelously for this battle royale with Goliath. In the wilderness, David absorbed valuable lessons when it came to engaging a dangerous foe one-on-one. He was fast—he could chase down a lion or a bear, slowed by carrying a sheep in its mouth. David learned to rush at a predator, to take the initiative. Then he discovered through brutal practice that he could kill a lion and a bear with his sling and a club and a knife. David fought and killed alpha predators in the wild and Goliath presented himself as the alpha of the Philistines. With these formidable skills, David approached Goliath. When David first saw Goliath and heard his taunts, he sized up his opponent. Goliath was *big*—which meant that he was likely slower than David. Seeing his size and strength, David knew that he did not want to get in close with Goliath or within range of his enormous weapons. But David didn't have to get close.

A weapon used in many parts of the ancient world, the sling allowed its user to inflict damage from a distance. The Hebrews employed groups of men with slings in their armies. Using this weapon, a stone weighing one-to-two pounds could be thrown over 200 yards by an experienced user. "Slingers" were known to be highly accurate at a close distance and the stones came so fast that they were nearly impossible to avoid. David spent days on end practicing with his sling while guarding his family's sheep. The skills necessary to win this confrontation infused David before he had ever heard of Goliath. David just applied these talents toward a new type of predator. Add to those competencies the cocksure nature of a teenager who's never tasted defeat and suddenly Goliath had his hands full.

Your past prepares you for your future. Your past comes into play in the challenges of your present. Your past matters and many of your greatest strengths grew out of earlier experiences. Your culture matters to your leadership. Your ethnicity matters. All are important and all influence you deeply. Embrace it. David stepped onto the stage as a Hebrew shepherd boy and he stepped off as a national hero. His background prepared him. How has your background prepared you? You have strengths that grew in you from your culture and your home. It may be a powerful sense of family, or a strong work ethic, or a sense of compassion for the less fortunate. Perhaps an enthusiasm for learning or the ability to embrace change developed along the way within you? Wherever you are from, your culture and your ethnicity and your family instilled strengths and skills within you. Do not overlook them. A leader develops awareness of the lessons learned earlier in life and thoughtfully considers how these lessons carry influence today.

You know how Goliath's story ends. David rushed toward him, got all his weight and momentum into his throw, and launched the deadly projectile like a bullet. The last thing to cross Goliath's mind, quite literally, was a stone. After Goliath collapsed, David killed him with his own sword and cut off his head. I wonder why we don't see pictures of that in Sunday School? David's butchery of Goliath started a rout as the Hebrews followed him onto the field and the Philistine lines collapsed. Israel won the victory, all thanks to the way God orchestrated events and developed a shepherd into a warrior. Forever the world will remember and refer to David and Goliath.

What about you? What abilities exist from your past, perhaps overlooked or lying dormant, that could influence your present situation? What part of your story might you be afraid to face, or to embrace? Where might you apply your lessons from your past? We all face Goliaths, so what weapons and skills and lessons aid you as you run to the battle? God gave you your past for a reason. Think on it and learn from it. Let your past help you become the leader God wants you to be.

CHAPTER TEN

I SAMUEL 25

Nabal and Abigail were one of those couples that leave you scratching your head. How did that crabby old man marry such an attractive young woman? Nabal's name means "fool," and he was certainly brutish and surly and self-centered. Likely this was a nickname, one he earned from people who worked for him and around him over the years, because what parents would actually name their child "fool?" Nabal was distinctly unpleasant and proved the accuracy of his name, as we will soon appreciate. His unfortunate wife, Abigail, was cut from a different cloth. Intelligent and beautiful, a killer combination in any culture at any time in history, Abigail appeared way too high class for Nabal. How did she come to marry such a man? It was not her choice. Nabal was wealthy, Abigail was good-looking. The match served her family by adding a rich new relation. Marriage served Nabal with an appealing young wife. The only person it did not serve so well was Abigail. She was stuck, but she was clever.

Into this awkward situation arrived a young warrior, on the run from an unrighteous ruler. David avoided Saul by hiding in the wilderness with his lively band of fighters. While constantly on the move to stay undetected, David and his men came into contact with Nabal's servants. David's men treated these servants kindly, not taking anything that was not offered and protecting them and their property. David's men acted respectfully towards Nabal's servants, above and beyond what was expected. In doing so, David's men won the friendship and loyalty of these servants and Nabal himself prospered due to this kindness.

David, with lots of hungry mouths to feed, sent a delegation to Nabal to request supplies. Because of the honorable treatment of his servants and considering his great wealth, the expectation was that Nabal would show gratitude and grant David's request. One good deed deserves another. Thoughtlessly, Nabal rebuffed David's men, spoke to them condescendingly, and sent them away empty-handed. Nabal proved the truth behind his nickname. David heard of the rebuke and was enraged. Still a young and developing leader, David solved problems with force. Mad as a hornet, he led 400 of his warriors to settle the score with Nabal. Nothing good was about to happen.

Then wisdom arrived. Abigail, the intelligent half of the couple, heard of the situation and responded decisively. She led a delegation to meet David and his mob. Abigail brought the two things necessary to turn David from his vicious plan: lots and lots of food and even more compliments, kind words, and apologies. And perhaps her beauty helped David pause and reassess the situation. As shallow as it may be, flattery from a beautiful woman has calmed the anger of many a man over the centuries.

David blessed Abigail for her good judgment. Abigail stopped the slaughter of her husband's servants, guilty only of working for a fool. On a larger scale, Abigail stopped David from an impulsive act that could have influenced his future kingship. Perhaps the Lord would have turned away from David, as he did Saul, for killing so many innocent people? David, Nabal, the servants and David's men—everyone benefited from Abigail's discernment and quick thinking.

Ironically, all this happened behind Nabal's back. When Abigail told him what she did and how close David had come to wiping them out, Nabal's heart seized up and he died a few days later. Good riddance—Israel could do with one less fool. David heard of Nabal's death and quickly sent a marriage proposal to the widow Abigail, which she immediately accepted. From the wife of a fool to the wife of a king, Abigail's fortunes reversed overnight.

Leadership involves discernment. Nabal had none. He either could not see, or refused to see, what was plain to everyone else. To rebuke David was to court disaster. Nabal lived a cruel and miserly life from which no one benefited. As you make your way in this world, you will meet and work with people like Nabal. You may even work for some, which will prove to be an exasperating experience. If this is the case, actively look for a way out. Your situation will not improve without outside intervention. Do all you can to avoid the "Nabals," the fools you encounter in life. Separate yourself from them as much as possible. A true fool refuses to be rehabilitated.

Let me share with you frankly, even though it may seem harsh. As a leader, if you find a Nabal working for you, then you need to act. Do not offer a fool either people to supervise or resources to squander. Do not give them a platform to represent you or your organization. Think long and hard about how you can fire them or demote them to a place they can do no harm. Seriously. The Apostle Paul cautions us in 2 Corinthians 11 not to "suffer a fool," or in other words, do not put up with their actions or attitudes. The book of Proverbs speaks often of fools and the havoc they cause. Proverbs 26:6 warns us that "sending a message by the hands of a fool is like cutting off one's feet or drinking poison." As a leader, realize that it is your job to deal with fools. Another sound bite from Proverbs 20:26 makes this clear: "After careful scrutiny, a wise leader makes a clean sweep of rebels and dolts" (see *The Message* version of Proverbs for more plain language regarding fools). Everyone will thank you. A fool's influence spreads farther that you realize. Talented people avoid and often leave an organization that allows a fool's influence. Considerable good does not happen when a fool's hand it at the helm.

Much better, pray for, seek out, hire, promote, and elevate people like Abigail within your sphere of influence. These are life-giving people and everyone around them benefits from their wisdom. The Lord blesses their kindness and judgment. Look for people of discernment, who read what's going on around them and who exhibit positivity. Leaders who recruit and bring on people like Abigail build powerful teams and develop organizations that bless the world.

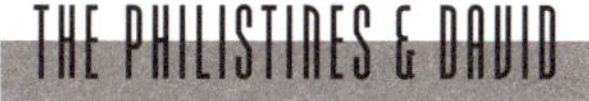

CHAPTER ELEVEN

I CHRONICLES 14

Sometimes you get what you want only to realize that what you wanted was way more than you could handle. Such was the case with the Philistines, who felt like David's victory over Goliath was a fluke and now that David operated as king, they ached to go teach him a lesson. It's easy to miss, so pay attention to this line found in 1 Chronicles 14:8: "When the Philistines heard that David had been anointed king over all Israel, they went up in *full force* to search for him. But David heard about it and went out to meet them" (emphasis mine). The Philistines in fully engaged mode would have been a sight to see. They raised warriors and fought continually. The Israelites served as their mortal enemies ever since Joshua led the Egyptian exiles into their promised land. This expedition was no lark. The Philistines prepared extensively and put their strongest pieces into play. "Full force" equaled all in. Sensing a weakness in an inexperienced king who had not yet consolidated power, the Philistine rulers sought to strike a blow to Israel that swung the pendulum of dominance back in their direction. Though it's barely mentioned in Scripture, this campaign seriously tested David's new administration. A superior army hurtled toward a young king. If David were defeated, the nation faced months or years of fighting. Much worse, if David were killed or captured, Israel would be leaderless and again under the boots of the Philistines.

David responded in his typical fashion. Without hesitation he left to face the invading force. Hunted by an invading army bent on your destruction? Perfect. In David's mind this means that we have them where we want them and now we can deal with this group of cutthroats once and for all. The same spirit that pushed David to run toward Goliath now drove him toward the Philistine army, hunting the hunters. Much to their dismay, the Philistines found who they came looking for. The ongoing battle developed into such a rout that the Philistines fled in panic, discarding anything weighing them down, including their idols. No match for the living God, David burned these "gods" as the mere pieces of wood and metal they turned out to be.

A leader acts. A leader wades into difficult situations. A leader listens to the Lord and moves decisively. Opportunity lives behind difficulty. Strength and maturity and wisdom grow due to going through the storms, not around them. The Lord can act through a leader who moves. You may not see the horizon, but the Lord does. When problems appear, when challenges arise, when Philistines march into your lands, get up and meet them face-to-face. When you do, the Lord can break out and the rout can take place. Hiding solves nothing. Rather than vacillate, step out and give the Lord the chance to work.

 THE QUEEN OF SHEBA

1 KINGS 10
2 CHRONICLES 9

The journey from Central Africa to the Middle East felt like forever. After so many weeks, everything smelled and tasted of camel. Even riding in the royal coach brought the growth of calluses in hard-to-describe places. Travel at the speed of camel left plenty to be desired, but the stories of the magnificent king of Israel and the splendor of his kingdom had reached the queen's ears. Solomon possessed great wealth and wisdom, and more intriguingly, tales told of his uncommon connection with his God stirred her heart.

Solomon was the wisest and wealthiest king in the history of Israel. Even today, three thousand years later, you'll read someone referred to as having "wisdom like Solomon." His reputation covered the ancient world. If you recall the story in 1 Kings 3, Solomon asked the Lord not for power or wealth or longevity, but for wisdom and discernment as he led the people as their new king. This request pleased the Lord and so God granted Solomon all of the above, in abundance. (Note to self: when leading, consider asking God for wisdom and understanding, rather than a robust budget or a splashier platform. Just a thought.)

Solomon's fame spread far and wide. Crowds flocked from Israel and the surrounding nations to hear his wisdom and witness the growing splendor of his kingdom. Carried by traders and itinerants, these stories spread to the heart of Africa, all the way to the court of the Queen of Sheba. A woman of abundant wealth and power, her neighboring territories held no special interest to her. Solomon, a wise king, wealthy beyond comprehension and a man with a special connection to God—now that was too much to ignore. Meeting Solomon consumed her thoughts. The planning began and the camels were mustered. She set out on this long and arduous journey, carrying gifts of tremendous value, surrounded by an army—all in order to see if the stories of the legendary king were true. She came not only to see, but also to question Solomon. I wonder what she planned to ask? Her questions are not recorded, but I'd imagine that she asked questions people have always struggled with, like "Why do bad things happen to good people?" Or, "How can I know God the way you do?" But also questions only another wise ruler could answer, possibly, "As a leader, who can I trust?"

Solomon satisfied the Queen with his answers. He explained everything. Solomon's wisdom, wealth, charisma and devotion to the Lord left her breathless. She got what she hoped for and so much more, realizing a depth in Solomon's insights she never heard from her royal advisors. After an extensive visit, she reluctantly left for home. The two powerful leaders exchanged gifts of phenomenal value, sealing their friendship.

What does a leader make of this story? The Queen of Sheba possessed power, riches, skills and wisdom of her own. Her aptitude for leading was apparent as a female ruler in a world of power-hungry men. Just like today, the strong preyed on the weak. The Queen was certainly not weak nor was she easy prey.

Why did she go meet Solomon? The Queen possessed a trait integral to leadership. The Queen was curious. She heard the stories of Solomon. No doubt, she sent trusted emissaries ahead of her to check out the facts. Their reports fueled her daydreams about this distant king and his God. Curiosity, and perhaps a bit of desperation, led her to Solomon. No one else could answer her difficult questions to her satisfaction. Perhaps she trusted no one close to her. Maybe, just maybe, Solomon could speak to her deep issues and maybe, just maybe, she could gain an understanding of this God who so blessed Israel.

Curiosity is an invaluable trait in a leader. Daydream, doodle, gaze out the window, and let your mind run. Make the effort to learn. Read books, take classes, visit foreign lands and always ask lots of questions. An active mind, an inquisitive bent, a wonder of what's around the corner helps you develop as a leader. You start to comprehend the world with more wisdom, to understand yourself with more clarity, and to appreciate God with more depth. Curiosity yields healthy discovery. Most wonderfully, as you chase your curiosity, from time to time you'll uncover something fresh and find yourself breathless.

1 KINGS 12

Have you ever had to give a speech? Most people hate public speaking. In fact, it's often number one on the lists of things people fear the most. The dread of getting up in front of people and saying something stupid keeps most of us in our seats. We don't want to look silly and we're afraid we'll blow it. Well, don't worry, because you cannot possibly do any worse than Rehoboam did when giving his first speech as the new king of Israel. Rarely have so few words cost a ruler so much. A fool and his kingdom were soon parted.

Rehoboam, son of the legendary Solomon, failed to inherit one ounce of his father's wisdom. Arrogant and spoiled, Rehoboam waited for years to grasp the reins of power. When his moment finally arrived, Rehoboam brought neither the sagacity of his father nor the communion with the Lord of his grandfather, David. Instead, he brought along his youthful advisors looking to take advantage of their new positions in the entourage of the king. With them came a certain expectation that the kingdom existed for their pleasure and the kingdom's subjects for their purposes. Raised in wealth and comfort, denied little in their adolescent lifestyles, these young men neither listened to sound advice nor dispensed any. Rejecting the guidance of Solomon's counselors, Rehoboam embraced the strategy of this youthful cohort. He chose poorly. Few lines in the Bible drip with such arrogance and disdain as Rehoboam's first speech to the nation's leaders. "My father made your yoke heavy, but I will add to your yoke. My father disciplined you with whips, but I will discipline you with scorpions." Not waiting around for the scorpions, ten of the twelve tribes of Israel immediately turned their backs on Rehoboam and crowned a new king. The magnificent kingdom of Israel, at the height of its glory and wealth, split forever after a single speech.

From this episode brought to us by Rehoboam and his gaggle of haughty advisors we find a lot to learn. First, nobody owes you his or her allegiance. You earn it. You may be given the title of "boss," but you earn the title of "leader." Second, learn to listen to the wise voices in your life. Often, older, more experienced women and men bring sound thinking into difficult decisions. Be sure to find and cultivate relationships with these types of mentors. Third, people asking honest questions, like we hear from the leaders of Israel, deserve thoughtful responses, not harsh edicts. Show some humility and enter into the world of those you're leading, or might soon be leading. Kindness and understanding will get you further than rudeness and bullying. From Rehoboam we learn how to fail as a leader when confronted with challenging questions from the people under our leadership. Do the opposite of Rehoboam. Listen, ask questions, and seek to understand. Request and consider the wisdom of others. Be thoughtful in your responses.

Finally, never promise a future filled with scorpions. People choose to whom they will give their good will and affections. Rehoboam's words were those of a slave master, not those of a visionary leader to follow into the future. People won't leave you over a bad speech. You'll be forgiven for stumbling during a talk. However, people will leave due to your bad character. Positive, humble, strong-hearted leaders are rare. Grow in these characteristics and you won't need to worry so much about your public speaking.

CHAPTER FOURTEEN

ELISHA & HIS SERVANT

2 KINGS 6

Up early in the morning and headed out the door, likely hustling to the outhouse, Elisha's servant stopped in his tracks and assessed his situation. The hills had eyes. Enemies all around. No way out. The army now camped at the gates of the city had come for only one person—his boss. The servant thought, "Elisha's going down and I'm going with him. Why did I take this job?" If ever there was a time to panic, this was it. "Alas, my master! What shall we do?" is how the Bible records his words of surprise and dismay. It was time to freak out.

Let's cycle back for a bit of context. Elisha, one of the great prophets of ancient Israel, lived during a time when the king of Israel and the king of Syria were constantly at war. Which doesn't feel much different than today. The king of Syria laid out all sorts of battle plans, but Elisha, informed by the Lord, kept tipping off the king of Israel. There existed a spy in the Syrian camp. The spy happened to be the Lord who whispered to Elisha the secret plans. What could the king of Syria do? He figured that while you cannot fight God, you could shut the mouth of his messenger. The king put together a large contingent of soldiers and cavalry and sent them to capture Elisha.

Now turn again to Elisha's servant, facing this calamity before his first cup of coffee, confronted with his fears of imminent capture, torture, imprisonment, and death. Elisha, however, saw the situation through a different lens. He told his servant, "Those who are with us are more than those who are with them." Elisha then prayed and his servant sensed the world anew, peering into an alternate dimension, a different edge of reality. He glimpsed the spiritual realm surrounding us. Like the shepherds who saw the heavens opened on the night of Christ's birth, and the Apostle Paul who described a great cloud of witnesses looking upon us, the servant suddenly and delightfully realized that another empire exists. He saw the mountains around them filled with horses and chariots of fire. Immediately, the Syrian army was not a threat, which Elisha proved as he soon dealt with their invasion. A spiritual realm most assuredly exists and is truly awesome. Wouldn't you love a glimpse?

What should a leader take away from this vignette about blazing chariots? First in my mind is that all leaders need help, like Elisha's manservant, who was sort of a cross between a personal assistant and a butler. Second and more importantly, a leader stays in tune with the surrounding spiritual realities. Engaged in the spiritual realm, a good leader reminds himself of this certainty. In our physical world, forgetting this truth happens easily, but our forgetting makes it no less real. When the servant panicked, Elisha remained cool and calm because Elisha saw the blazing chariots of God surrounding the now frail wagons of the Syrians. No contest. Third, a godly leader helps others grasp these hidden realities around them. Elisha injected fresh perspective when he prayed for the Lord to open his servant's eyes. Good leaders lavishly deliver vision. Spiritual leaders constantly remind people to observe the world using their own spiritual sight, to perceive the spiritual realm all around us. Elisha assured his servant, "Don't worry, there are more on our side than on their side," which remains a wonderful promise for anyone following the Lord. Psalm 24:1 reminds us that, "The earth is the Lord's and all it contains." Every place on this planet belongs to the Lord. That's reality. Take a look around. Could it be that the horizons around you are full of chariots and horses of fire? As you look on the seemingly insurmountable issues facing you today, you may be tempted to panic or to fold into yourself in fear or to give up in resignation. These are natural responses to an overwhelming world. Instead, repeat the prayer of Elisha and ask for eyes open to "those who are with us." A worthy leader comprehends spiritual reality and helps others yearn for it for themselves.

CHAPTER FIFTEEN

JEHOIDA & JOASH

2 CHRONICLES 22-24

Joash put up with one mean grandma. You may come from a dysfunctional family, but it's doubtful you come from a family as bad as Joash's. His disturbed kinfolk also happened to be the royal family of Judah, so the entire nation suffered along with the young Joash. The royals in Judah spread the pain all around.

Joash's father, Ahaziah, previously held the office of king. He was a lousy one as it turned out, and he lasted only a year on the throne before being murdered during an insurrection. Upon Ahaziah's death his mother, Athaliah, seized power in brutal fashion. She destroyed the rest of the royal family and murdered all the princes in the kingdom. Not exactly the "bake you some cookies then read you a story" kind of grandmother, she was more like Joseph Stalin in your kitchen. Targeted for murder like the rest of the royal heirs, Joash's aunt rescued him and hid him in a tucked-away bedroom. Joash went into hiding as a one-year-old baby and lived the next six years in that room, evading sweet grandma Athaliah.

Can you imagine? Just like a fairy tale, the evil queen reigns while the true king remains hidden away, growing up in the temple of God. Evil personified, if Athaliah discovered Joash she would kill him without hesitation. During these days of hiding, the true hero of this story emerged. Jehoiada, a leading priest and the husband of the woman who rescued Joash, patiently waited to take action. We should all be so lucky to have friends as wise and faithful as Jehoiada and his wife. All during the reign of Athaliah, Jehoiada delayed. He knew that the current situation was wrong and he suffered in silence as he served the malicious queen. But he could not address the situation until the boy king, Joash, grew older and the queen grew complacent. I'm guessing that he waited for other leaders of the nation to grow increasingly frustrated as well. Jehoiada guarded his secret, the little boy king, for six long years.

In year seven Jehoiada moved from silent observer to active revolutionary. Gathering a coalition of military and religious leaders, he led a coup to overturn the government. Jehoiada installed Joash as king and put the evil queen to death, ending her reign of terror. He set things right as he placed the true king on the throne. The scriptures tell us that "all the people of the land rejoiced and the city was quiet after Athaliah had been put to death with the sword." (FYI, when people rejoice after your leadership reign is over, you were doing something wrong.) Then they all lived happily ever after.

Well, not quite. The people of Judah did live happily for many years, experiencing a time of prosperity and peace. For at least twenty-five years, Joash reigned as a good and wise king with Jehoiada at this side. Joash started a family.

He restored the temple to its former glory and continually offered sacrifices to honor God. Under the leadership of Joash and his primary advisor, Jehoiada, the people flourished.

The value of mentors, of wise people around you, cannot be overstated. Leaders must surround themselves with good and wise people whenever possible. We need mentors who will tell us the truth and who will act when necessary. A worthy advisor helps you make good decisions and avoid mistakes. Sometimes a great mentor, as in this case, may save your life.

Jehoiada died old and full of years. Esteemed so highly for his service, Jehoiada received the ultimate privilege of burial with the kings in Jerusalem, an honor bestowed on only a few. Perhaps no one in the history of Judah and Israel served a king as wisely and as selflessly as Jehoiada did Joash. Only upon the death of Jehoiada do we see the extent of his hand of wisdom upon the king. Shortly after Jehoiada passed, Joash abandoned the temple and turned to other gods, committing great evils in the eyes of the Lord. God sent Zechariah, the son of Jehoiada, to warn the king of his fall from grace. Joash took Zechariah, the son of his mentor and protector, and stoned him to death. The writer of Chronicles tells us that "King Joash did not remember the kindness Zechariah's father, Jehoiada, had shown him." No kidding.

Joash flourished as king and led his nation well when a good man stood next to him. He followed God and the people prospered. When his wise mentor passed, Joash grew unhinged. He reverted to the leadership style of his grandmother and killed the son of his savior. A good guide, a wise voice in the ear of another person matters. It matters among royalty and among common folk. Crave wisdom. Seek it. Keep close to wise people. Allow them to mold you and move you to greater and higher places.

Stories with a twist fill the Bible. It's one reason I love reading it so much. As it turns out, the Lord eventually pivoted on Joash. God allowed the nation's enemies, the Arameans, to conquer Jerusalem. They killed the leaders and wounded Joash severely. After the enemy withdrew and while he still recovered from his wounds, Joash was assassinated in his bed, likely as a payback for murdering Zechariah. In a final indignity, now hated by the people of Judah, Joash was refused burial in the tombs of the kings. How far he fell. Jehoiada, the wise counselor, took the king's place of honor in the royal cemetery. Never overlook the fact that intelligent leaders listen to and apply input from discerning mentors. Our lives and the lives of those we love depend upon it.

2 CHRONICLES 32

The Assyrian army outside Jerusalem felt like a tidal wave cresting against the walls. No other city had survived their attacks. No previous gods rescued their people from these conquering warriors. Nothing and nobody slowed the steady march of Sennacherib, the Assyrian king, through the nation of Judah. What possibly could be done to stop them? Would the meager defensive preparations hold? For how long? All these thoughts and more rolled through the mind of Hezekiah, the king of Judah, as he stood on the wall and gazed at this vast collection of men and war machinery before him. All of them there to end his life and to destroy Jerusalem.

In this dark hour, with the barbarians at the gate, Hezekiah gave a speech. He assembled the people and told them, "Be strong and courageous. Do not be afraid or discouraged because of the King of Assyria and the vast army with him, for there is a greater power with us than with him. With him is only the arm of flesh, but with us is the Lord our God to help us and to fight our battles." That's it. Short and to the point. How did the besieged people respond? "And the people gained confidence from what Hezekiah the King of Judah said." Hezekiah's words, his trust in the Lord, his vision of who fights for the nation instilled confidence in these besieged citizens. His speech helped them to stand firm in the face of an overwhelming force. A leader motivates. A leader may not be a gifted speaker or a talented writer, but a leader figures out how to motivate his followers to a desired end.

In this case of Hezekiah, his well-spoken words come at just the right time. As we watch the story unfold, the Lord responded to Hezekiah's faith and the blasphemy of Sennacherib by sending an angel who wiped out every fighting man of Assyria. The beaten king withdrew in shame and returned home where his sons assassinated him in the temple of his god. The Lord proves a point like no other. No arm of flesh stands a chance against the Lord. Mock the living God? Never a good idea. Wiser to pray and trust the Lord like Hezekiah.

Also, like Hezekiah, better to transfer that trust to others. "The people gained confidence from what Hezekiah said." Have you ever been the recipient of a well-spoken word? Perhaps a compliment when you needed it most, or a note of courage when afraid? How about a good yelling from a coach, or a challenge to excel from a teacher? A leader motivates. An influential leader motivates in such a way that the "people gain confidence." Confidence breeds action. Confidence is contagious. Confidence paired with the Lord wins battles. Learn to instill confidence in others as you lead. Better yet, learn to instill confidence in the Lord among those you lead and you might just change the world.

CHAPTER SEVENTEEN

NEHEMIAH 1-6

Some afternoons, when the time for the wine tasting arrived, nothing felt unusual at all. Occasionally, he could actually enjoy sipping the finest wines gathered from the diverse regions of the empire and beyond, especially appreciating those from the far-off vineyards in the south of Europe. But most days it was hard to escape the thought that maybe this would be the day. Perhaps earlier this morning, someone had slipped something poisonous into the vat and, as the first taster, Nehemiah might end up being the one getting killed. He would die so that the king might live.

Nehemiah served as cupbearer for the king. While not in a position of leadership, Nehemiah daily served the most powerful man alive, King Artaxerxes of the Medes and Persians. The cupbearer did not need to be a warrior or a poet, but the cupbearer absolutely had to be trustworthy since he protected the king from an assassin poisoning his drink. Nehemiah literally drank with the king every day, putting his life at risk with every sip. From this valuable service developed a priceless commodity, the listening ear and good will of the most powerful man on earth.

Nehemiah curried the king's favor because Nehemiah harbored an audacious plan in his heart. Nehemiah yearned to return and rebuild the walls of Jerusalem, and he could not accomplish this massive project without the blessing and support of Artaxerxes. Jerusalem, the city of David, conquered years before, lay vulnerable behind shattered walls. Ruined and insignificant, why would Artaxerxes wish to spend any of the royal assets in a rebuilding effort?

Before confronting the seemingly impossible task of appealing to the king's judgment, Nehemiah first approached the true King: He prayed. In fact, Nehemiah fasted and prayed before the Lord for days. He confessed the sins of the people of Israel to the Lord and asked for forgiveness. Nehemiah pled for favor with Artaxerxes, knowing he would soon approach the king regarding his plan. Nehemiah expressed his dependence on the Lord. *A leader prays.*

Along with praying, Nehemiah did his homework before asking specifically for all he wanted. One day, while Nehemiah served the king wine, Artaxerxes noticed that his cupbearer was sad. The king was concerned for his trusted servant and so asked what bothered him. Just a side note: Do your work well and others will value, appreciate and listen to you. Nehemiah recognized his chance and did not miss out on the opportunity. He laid out all he was thinking to the king—his idea to go back to Jerusalem and rebuild the walls of the city. Furthermore, Nehemiah explained to the king all the logistics necessary for the success of the plan. Nehemiah asked for letters from the king's hand, addressed to the officials over the region surrounding Jerusalem, stipulating the permission for Nehemiah to be there, to rebuild the walls and to be given, free of charge, all the necessary building materials. Nehemiah waited for the right time to speak to the king, but as he waited, he prayed and studied and planned. Not only did Artaxerxes say yes to all these requests, as a hint to how much he valued Nehemiah, he threw in a detachment of cavalry and their officers to accompany Nehemiah's entourage. Nehemiah walked into work that day with a dream, and he walked out of the palace as the emissary of the king. *A leader prepares.*

In reading the rest of the story, you realize that it's one thing to go before the king to get permission to act, but it's quite another thing to travel a thousand miles away to rebuild a wall that many did not want to see rebuilt. I heard an old expression in China years ago, when discussing the problems a central government faces in putting policies in effect across that broad country: "The emperor is far away and the mountains are tall." Artaxerxes, Nehemiah's emperor and advocate, lived far away. Nehemiah confronted his adversaries and their roadblocks continually. Nehemiah endured to build his wall in the face of this opposition and hostility. At one point, fearing an attack by his enemies, Nehemiah ordered half the people laboring to stand guard while the other half worked, "doing the work with one hand and holding a weapon with the other." The entire population of the city joined in the rebuilding and toiled ever prepared to defend themselves. This basically doubled the time necessary to complete the task, but despite the constant threat of violence (or perhaps because of it) the people restored the walls of Jerusalem. *A leader perseveres.*

Nehemiah practiced the discipline of prayer, which moved the heart of God, who in turn softened the heart of the king. Nehemiah strategized, designed and calculated before speaking to Artaxerxes. He knew what he needed and what he would ask for if given the chance. Nehemiah understood that the king was the only person who could grant his request and he readied himself for this crucial conversation. Upon riding into Jerusalem, the enormity of the task and the schemes of his enemies threatened to crush Nehemiah. It required courage and long days and encouraging words and sore backs and shifts in plans and sharpening old swords and tracking myriads of details to get this job done. Few would even attempt rebuilding such a huge structure while remaining vigilant to the threat of violence. Nehemiah stuck it out and won the day. Leaders pray. Leaders prepare. Leaders persevere. When this happens, others expectantly join in and build towards significance.

CHAPTER EIGHTEEN

ESTHER 1-10

Queen Esther stood outside the door to the throne room, apprehensive yet resolute. Although his favorite, appearing before the king without a summons was unprecedented. A smile or a scowl could be the difference between life as the queen of an empire or banishment, or even worse. Esther certainly did not want to share the fate of the former queen, whom she recently replaced. But Esther stood as the only person in the kingdom that might possibly convince the king to prevent the massacre of thousands of innocents and stop a genocide. She placed her life on the line for her people, because, if not her, then who? As her uncle reminded her, perhaps she was born and became queen "for such a time as this."

Esther's story reads like a novel that you can't put down. It starts out as a rags to riches story, an immigrant's rise to power. Her upswing was made possible because the former queen refused to answer the summons of her husband, King Xerxes. Fearful that the queen's actions would set a bad precedent for the women of the empire (true male privilege of the highest order), the king's advisors encouraged him to dump the old queen and find a new one. Fearing open revolt and cold dinners, the king deposed Queen Vashti and went in search for a new queen. Somewhat enthusiastically, it appears. To find his new queen, Xerxes held an ancient pageant, gathering beautiful women from all across his kingdom. The one who pleased him the most would become queen. It was a good gig, the life of an ancient, all-powerful ruler, if you could get it. Esther, a Jewish immigrant, delighted the king and so became queen. From an unknown girl living in her uncle's back room to the king's palace, Esther rocketed to the empire's highest social strata. But not all was rosy in the royal household.

One of the king's advisors, a despicable character named Haman, got sideways with Mordecai, Esther's uncle, when Mordecai refused to bow to Haman on the street one afternoon. The vain Haman burned for revenge. He schemed not only to kill Mordecai, but to put to death all of Mordecai's people, the Jews living in exile throughout the entire kingdom. He convinced the king of the soundness of his idea and so set the plot in motion.

Let's pause and take stock of King Xerxes. So far, we've seen him fire queen Vashti for her insolence. Then he took several weeks to search for a new queen, which primarily involved bedding a fresh virgin every night. Next, one of his advisors hatched a plan to murder a peaceful segment of his population and the king agreed without a question or a second thought. Xerxes was either mad or evil. Regardless, he appears easily and dangerously swayed by whoever whispers into his ear last. Pity the people ruled by such a fool.

Back to Esther. As her uncle carefully explained, she

faced death from Haman's scheme as sure as all the other Jews. Don't think that Haman will spare any Jew—even the Queen—and don't hope things just work out on their own. To stay quiet meant disaster. Esther must expose this conspiracy to the king. As Uncle Mordecai told her, "Who knows, whether you have not come to the kingdom for such a time as this?" Mordecai believed that the Lord has placed Esther in a position of power to save the Jews or die trying. Esther stepped forward, knocked on Xerxes's door and crossed the threshold in faith. The king extended his scepter to Esther and so she saved her people. You should read the full story in her book. Not only are the Jews saved, but Haman receives his due. He is killed – stuck on a spit – and Mordecai replaces him as chief advisor to the king. Everyone in the land benefits from Mordecai's wisdom for years to come. Esther saves the day by stepping into her fears with bravery and trust in the Lord.

What does Esther teach us about leadership? First, you are not in the position you are in by accident. Who knows why the Lord has you there? Mordecai nor Esther nor any of the Jewish exiles foresaw the looming genocide promoted by Haman. The catastrophe materialized before they could react. Only Esther could affect the outcome and then only by gambling her position and her physical safety, essentially jeopardizing all she had. What, to you, is worth risking everything? What are you willing to risk under dire circumstances? What are you willing to risk under normal circumstances? Are you willing to risk at all, or are you more likely to keep your head down and avoid conflict? Think about it. Why are you leading?

The second lesson from Queen Esther involves fear. The best way to deal with fear is to step toward it. Fear causes reticence and hesitation. Move and you start to break the grip of fear. Fear is better faced than evaded.

Third, your failure to act might lead to drastic consequences. Perhaps over the horizon, unbeknownst to you, wait either detrimental consequences or encouraging opportunities that depend on your actions. To do nothing is a feeble choice. Sins of omission are just as valid as sins of commission. If you are afraid to move ahead, then perhaps it's time to step aside and let someone else lead. No one benefits from an indecisive leader.

The Jews needed Esther to step toward the king and save their lives. The world needs you to step forward and change lives. Today challenges await, good and evil hang in the balance, and resilient leaders are few. Our world needs you to lead. Perhaps you are where you are for "such a time as this."

 THE SHEPHERD

PSALM 23

The Lord is my shepherd;
I shall not want.
He makes me to lie down in green pastures;
He leads me beside the still waters.
He restores my soul;
He leads me in the paths of righteousness
For his name's sake.
Yea, though I walk through the valley of the shadow of death,
I will fear no evil;
For you are with me;
Your rod and your staff, they comfort me.
You prepare a table before me in the presence of my enemies;
You anoint my head with oil;
My cup runs over.
Surely goodness and mercy shall follow me all the days of my life;
And I will dwell in the house of the Lord forever.

You've just read the most recognized and beloved passage

found in the Bible, and one of the most comforting pieces of literature in human history. It's often read at memorials and funerals as a reminder for those grieving the loss of a loved one that we follow a worthy shepherd, one we can trust and approach for comfort. Beyond that, this Psalm endures to remind all of us about the shepherd guiding us.

Psalm 23 holds distinct lessons for a leader. First, the Lord is our shepherd, and the Lord is the shepherd of others as well. The Lord is the ultimate shepherd. Not me. Not you. Sometimes we need to remember this reality when we attempt to control people. It's the Lord who controls events and circumstances, nations and leaders. Not me. Not you. Take a closer look at the psalms that bookend the twenty-third. The end of Psalm 22 tells us, "Dominion belongs to the Lord and he rules the nations...posterity will serve him; future generations will be told about the Lord. They will proclaim his righteousness, declaring to a people yet unborn; he has done it!" (Psalm 22:28-31). The Lords rules the nations, he is in charge and the entire world will one day know it. No need for us to shoulder the weight of the world, God's shoulders are broad enough.

Now observe the start of Psalm 24: "The earth is the Lord's and everything in it, the world and all who live upon it" (Psalm 24:1). The Lord owns it all. In another passage the psalmist tells us that the Lord owns "the cattle on a thousand hills." If you want a good picture of the cattle the Lord owns, drive through the Flint Hills of Kansas or the Ozark Mountains of Missouri. There you will appreciate rise after rise of grazing cattle, a beautiful reminder of the Lord's goodness. The Lord doesn't just own the cattle, but the Lord owns the hills as well, and the grass and the trees and the ponds and the prairie dogs. Everything. The earth is the

Lord's and everything in it. That's all encompassing. But it doesn't stop with the flora and fauna. The Lord owns all who live upon the earth. Every person belongs to the Lord, whether they know it or not.

The Lord cares for people much more than you or I do—and much, much more than we are even capable of doing. The shepherd is good in unfathomable ways. We can trust him, we can rest in him and we can rely on him. Do the best you can, knowing that the shepherd is at work in ways you cannot see. The shepherd owns all the land and controls all the water. He opens and closes the gates. He designs the grass to grow. He sprinkles the dew. You can rely on the shepherd.

Psalm 23 reminds us of God's presence. God genuinely surrounds us! This astonishing thought terrifies and invigorates. God's presence settles over every endeavor, which does not mean that God blesses or condones every endeavor, but it does mean that a leader remembers the shepherd's presence. "The Lord is my shepherd" should both comfort and provoke. Graze on that thought for a while.

A leader should reflect on the truth that he also serves in the role of a shepherd. If you are guiding and directing others, you are proceeding in the way of the shepherd. You may be God's appointed shepherd for this time and this place in the lives of the people you are leading. Notice the language as you consider your role as a leader. The shepherd "leads to quiet waters...restores...comforts...prepares a table." As a shepherd, you are to care for your people. You lead them tenderly to restoration in the Lord. You help them know the good shepherd.

The rest of the Psalm sets a different tone: "walk through the valley of the shadow of death...prepare a table in the presence of my enemies...fear no evil." You also must lead your people courageously. Lead them out to face the world with all the challenges you know await. You must guide them through difficult circumstances, even perilous situations at times. Evil exists, whether the sexual exploitation of children or the abject poverty of millions or the murder of innocents by fanatical religious zealots or the untimely death of a loved one. You must lead into and through these chasms. The good shepherd is with you. Decent people will grow fearful in the face of such dreadfulness. They will draw back, turn around, hunker down and quit. Shepherd them. Move forward alongside them, facing the fray, walking closely with the good shepherd through the valley of the shadow of death. Whether leading into a place of peace, or out to a place of conflict, remind people of the good shepherd. Lead people to the savior, to Jesus, every day.

As you consider this passage, let me offer you three uncommon words that I came across years ago to help me remember the leadership principles found within. These three particular words happen to be in Latin, which not only will help your recall, but will also impress your friends: *cura, animos, redemptor*. *Cura* means care. Care for the people under your charge. Steer them to places of rest and reflection. Help nurture them in spirit and body. *Animos* means courage. Lead courageously. Lead from the front. Push from behind. Take people to places they would not go without a guide. *Redemptor* means redeemer. Escort your people to the Redeemer. They need Jesus, just as all peoples around the world need him. *Cura, Animos, Redemptor*. I'm not one for tattoos, but if you're looking for a phrase to immortalize on your body, you could do worse. Regardless of where you jot it down, whether in your Bible or on your chest, record these words somewhere important then let them guide your leadership philosophy.

One final thought. When you let the good shepherd lead you, and you lead others to the good shepherd, you are doing the right thing. Rest assured in that truth. You can do no better. You are doing people good. When their cup overflows and goodness and mercy follows them, they will understand. Remember that as you lead, the best path follows closely behind the steps of the good shepherd.

CHAPTER TWENTY

SHADRACH, MESHACH & ABEDNEGO

DANIEL 3

The golden statue gleamed magnificently under the broad sun. The colossal image turned out better than imagined, and the man doing the imagining never struggled with small ideas. Only a guy with a robust self-image would build a golden figure of himself and command everyone to bow down and worship. As a conqueror and a sovereign, Nebuchadnezzar definitely had things going his way. To show the world his glory and wealth, Nebuchadnezzar commissioned a gilded doppelgänger. Ninety feet tall and covered with pure gold, the effigy represented the epitome of Nebuchadnezzar's reign. The fact that the king forced everyone to bow and worship proved the height of his power and egotism.

Everyone bowed. True believers or not, when the choices placed before the crowd involved either bowing down and worshipping or burning alive in a furnace, everyone went to their knees, even if they felt this was an exercise in idiocy. Why anger the king when you don't have to? Just bow down,

get it over with and go back to your life. Three men, however, decided against this option. Shadrach, Meshach and
Abednego served the king as Jewish captives. Monarchs
often took talented young people from conquered nations
into their service. They lived a fortunate life compared to the
rest of their fellow captives. But even in their privilege, with
so much to lose, Shadrach, Meshach and Abednego refused
to bow to a foreign god. They bowed only to the one true
God. Quickly, some of their coworkers accused them before
the king, likely out of jealousy or a desire for their position
in the government hierarchy. As a result, Nebuchadnezzar
discovered that not everyone participated fully in the worship services he so elaborately planned.

The furious king ordered Shadrach, Meshach and
Abednego to be brought before him. Nothing like the mania
of a Middle-Eastern despot to lubricate the wheels of state.
Nebuchadnezzar delineated the situation once again with
the three young holdouts, making it crystal clear that when
the band plays, it's time to go to your knees. No more confusion, no more benefit of the doubt. One aspect of this story
that's important to note is that these young men, described
as "exceptional," served as reliable and faithful servants.
Likely the king hated to lose such good young leaders,
so he pulled them in for a little chat to clear things up.
Nebuchadnezzar spoke clearly so there would be no mis-
understanding. If you choose to not worship my god, then
you've chosen your own death, roasted alive while we all
watch.

You have to wonder what went through the minds of
Shadrach, Meshach and Abednego as they absorbed this lecture from the disturbed king. Did the temptation to compromise cross their minds? How many other Jews had already

gone to their knees? Who would have blamed the three if they chose to bow and live to fight another day? Not the king and not anyone else. As Nebuchadnezzar laid the options before these young men, he tipped his hand as to his belief in the power of the gods when he uttered, "who is the god who will deliver you out of my hands?" The king believed in the power he could see and the influence he could yield. His ninety-foot tall statue existed not to create worshipful hearts in his subjects, but to control them and bend them to his will. The gods were created to be used by great men like Nebuchadnezzar. Gods don't control men, rather men control the gods.

If Shadrach, Meshach and Abednego feared the king or cowered in intimidation, even for a second, we don't see it. Perhaps something in Nebuchadnezzar's delivery flipped a switch in these young men that steeled their consciousness and hardened their resolve. Their response showed no hesitation or guesswork. No compromise. No retreat. No bowing.

The retort Shadrach, Meshach and Abednego offered to King Nebuchadnezzar, the most powerful man in the world, echoes through Scripture. No one spoke this way to such a king and lived. I picture it like this: Shadrach, Meshach and Abednego before Nebuchadnezzar—they heard his argument and then offered their response. With downcast eyes, they clarified the belief that God can save them if he wants—he's that powerful. Nebuchadnezzar knew that no god could save anyone he put in the furnace, but to his bewilderment, the three young men then raised their heads, looked the king in the eyes, and explained calmly that even if God did not save them, "let it be known to you, O king, that we will not serve your gods or worship the golden image you have set up."

Nebuchadnezzar erupted. No one talked to him this way. No one turned down his favor. Who were these men who had the gall to defy him like this? This may be the greatest line in all of history spoken to a tyrant. Sometimes a leader must stand on principle. Over the centuries, men and women confronted similar decisions. Shadrach, Meshach and Abednego formulated their decision well before going into the king's presence. They stood resolute, even though it could cost them their lives.

A leader needs bedrock principles for which they would die. Only a few and only the most important, but every true leader embraces such life-directing beliefs. Nebuchadnezzar, a leader corrupted by power and pride, met three young men holding deep wells of faith and courage, and he tried to kill them. The world continually develops a crop of leaders like Nebuchadnezzar, tyrants like Nero, Hitler, or Pol Pot, leaders willing to destroy people to get what they want. Pray that you are spared from living under such a curse and pray for those who are not so fortunate.

Nebuchadnezzar amped up the furnace seven times hotter than normal, so hot that the Babylonian guards who tossed in Shadrach, Meshach and Abednego perished from the heat. The king sat back to watch the spectacle and to enjoy the lesson he planned to send to his court and his kingdom—but astonishingly, impossibly, the men did not burn. They walked in the midst of the fire, unaffected by the blaze and were actually joined by a fourth man who seemed to speak to them. Most Bible scholars believe this fourth man was Jesus Christ, appearing in the flesh years before his birth.

Shadrach, Meshach and Abednego strolled out of the furnace unsinged, bearing no evidence of their experience in a fiery hell, not even a whiff of smoke on their robes. Astounded, Nebuchadnezzar now embraced the God who saves. His world twisted upside down due to this encounter with the living God. Nebuchadnezzar responded with the zealous faith of the newly converted, one who also happened to be an all-powerful emperor. He proclaimed that anyone saying anything against the God of Shadrach, Meshach and Abednego would be torn limb from limb and their house laid to waste. While his methodology remained barbaric, Nebuchadnezzar's fledgling faith was in the right place, focused on the one true God who rescued from certain death.

Those who follow the Lord will eventually bump into tyrants of some type. Rarely as terrible as Nebuchadnezzar; more commonly of the petty type. All will call you to compromise, to give up something of your commitment to the Lord in order to get along with their agenda. Don't do it. Know the lines you won't cross. Don't fear taking a stand. The world yearns for leaders standing firm. The Lord walks with you in your furnace. Just make sure you get thrown in for the right reason.

DANIEL 6

Daniel broke the law. Of this there was no doubt. There was a rigged decree passed in an underhanded way aimed specifically at Daniel by envious foes—but it was still the law. Wrong and unenforceable, this law only had to accomplish one purpose: to silence Daniel permanently.

Daniel served as a top leader in the administration of Darius, king of Persia. Daniel so excelled in his job that Darius planned to put him in charge of all the other officials in the kingdom. At the news of this idea, jealousy raised her foul head and a group of overlooked officials, soon to be subservient to Daniel, sought to destroy the king's new favorite. They knew exactly where to strike and designed an ingenious plan, lovely in its simplicity and deception. First, they maneuvered the king into considering legislation stating that for thirty days only Darius could receive prayers of any kind. Yielding to his pride and apparently not consulting his intellect, the all-powerful monarch signed the petition, making it the irrevocable law of the land—and all in the absence of his top advisor, Daniel, of course.

Next happened one of the bravest acts recorded in the Bible. When Daniel discovered the document had been signed, understanding that is was now illegal and punishable by death to pray to anyone besides the king for thirty days, Daniel went straight home, walked up the stairs, opened his window that faced toward Jerusalem, got down on his knees and prayed to God. Not to Darius. In fact, Daniel prayed three times that day, in full view of anyone who happened to look his way. Daniel willingly disobeyed the king and his law. Daniel prayed to God, knowing that his actions could lead to a grisly death in a den of lions.

What does a leader take from the example of Daniel? For one, there are times when a leader should compromise and there are times to stand firm. Daniel saw this as a time to openly proclaim his faith in God. Daniel could have prayed for the next month with his windows closed and in the privacy of his bedroom. It was only thirty days, a small concession in the larger scheme of life. Better to give in, to bend a little, to live and influence the king for years to come rather than face the lions. Apparently this type of rational thinking never registered with Daniel. With no hesitation, he walked home, threw open the shutters and prayed, all in defiance of the king and his evil advisors, lions be damned.

Sometimes leaders must act this way. This law was obviously wrong. The king did not deserve to receive the prayers of the people. The citizens of his kingdom, especially the Jewish remnant of the population, should not have been forced to compromise their faith in God. This law created a situation where anyone could be put to death on the word of anyone else: a resentful neighbor or manipulative employee, perhaps. It was simply an unworkable and bad law. Had

Darius been a more thoughtful tyrant he would not have signed the bill.

Daniel prayed and was caught. Dragged before Darius, he was sentenced to a night with the lions. Despite the king's efforts the punishment was carried out. Which leads me to the question: If you are an all-powerful tyrant who wishes to be worshipped as a god, why can't you think of a way to get Daniel out of this mess? Maybe write a new directive overruling the old law? Or simply remove the lions for the evening? Not sure Darius thought deeply about much of anything. (Lots of inbreeding in those ancient royal lines, you know.)

Daniel dropped into the pit but God restrained the lions. Darius, who truly valued Daniel, spent a sleepless night and rushed to the door of the cave early the next morning. On finding Daniel alive, Darius celebrated in truly tyrannical fashion by throwing all of Daniel's accusers and their families to the lions where they were immediately devoured. Perhaps chastened at his prideful behavior in thinking he was a god, Darius sent an edict throughout his dominions. He ordered all people to "tremble and fear before the God of Daniel, the living God, enduring forever." Not only is Daniel saved and the evildoers punished, but all of the vast kingdom is introduced to the God who saves. History tells us that Daniel prospered throughout the reign of Darius and his successor.

A leader holds firm. A leader supports what is right despite the prevailing winds of public opinion. If asked to compromise the core of their faith, to worship and serve anything other than the Creator, a godly leader does not hesitate. Like Daniel, such a leader pulls up the shades, flings open the windows and takes a public stance no matter the consequences.

In some parts of the world, followers of Christ face death for taking a stand, just like Daniel. I've met some of them. We have no way of knowing how many Christ followers have gone to their graves because they refused to compromise their faith in Jesus. The numbers are vast and growing daily. In the West, believers rarely face death for their faith, but who knows what the future may bring? The tree that is the church, fertilized for centuries by the blood of martyrs, flourishes in a violent world. Even without violence, ostracism or social suicide or closed doors may come to those who speak for the Lord. Losing a promotion or even a job may result from taking a stand in the workplace. Friends and family may not understand, turning away. But the Lord understands and the Lord does not turn away. Along with the Lord, lots of solid believers, followers of Jesus, will understand, will be encouraged and will turn your way. It was not just the persecutors who noticed Daniel's prayers at that window. God-fearing neighbors noticed and prayed with him and understood the Lord in a new light. They told their children and grandchildren about Daniel. To this day, we still name our sons Daniel.

Daniel's faith turned the heart of a king who in turn proclaimed the truth of God to the edges of his kingdom. A leader obeys God first and then faces the consequences of doing so. By leading this way, you create ripple effects of faith that influence generations, much like Daniel and Darius and those hungry lions.

CHAPTER TWENTY-TWO

JESUS

MARK 10:35-42
JOHN 13:1-20

The string of disciples, walking the long road to Jerusalem, slowly stretched and the increasing distance between them offered the two brothers their opportunity. With no shame or self-doubt, they approached Jesus. The "Sons of Thunder," as their nickname tells us, were not the most subtle of questioners. James and John came to Jesus and said, "Teacher, we want you to do for us whatever we ask"—a wonderfully open-ended question, sort of like asking a genie for infinite wishes. Jesus, the patient rabbi, simply replied, "What do you want me to do for you?" Which drew out the real question these disciples were pondering as they walked.

James and John asked, "Let one of us sit at your right and the other at your left in your glory." Over several months, an accurate picture of the power of Jesus began to coalesce in the hearts and minds of the disciples. They realized, if only dimly at this point, that the teacher they followed possessed far more power than any mere man. Jesus, destined to reign in glory, held their futures as well. James and John did not want to miss out. They wanted a piece for themselves. How tempting must it have been for simple country fishermen to dream of reigning with Jesus in an eternal city, one far surpassing the magnificence of Jerusalem or even Rome. These were bold men and they seized their chance. Why not ask Jesus for more?

Surprisingly, Jesus did not rebuke them, but rather asked them if they thought they had what it takes. Could they "drink the cup" and "receive the baptism" that will come their way? James and John believed they could, but Jesus developed the conversation further by letting them peek into their future. They most certainly would "drink" and be "baptized," meaning that James and John would suffer for the kingdom of God. John's sip of the cup involved his exile and death on a lonely island and James's baptism led to being decapitated in Jerusalem, the first of Jesus's original disciples to be martyred. But where they sit in eternity was not up to Jesus. Those places were reserved for someone else.

James and John may seem presumptuous or arrogant to us today (the other disciples certainly felt so), but their questions reveal an attitude present in all of us. "What's in this for me?" The allure of power and reward in the mind of a leader draws out attitudes and actions that may surprise us. Leaders wield power in order to advance their agenda. History teaches that power helps and power hurts and, no matter how pure the heart, power eventually corrupts. This corrosive influence is why we constantly hear of leaders—political, business and non-profit—overstepping bounds. Whether it involves living in opulence or flaunting their position or simply treating people as *less than*, the world brings us example after example of power-hungry leaders. Paired nicely with power, like a fine wine with a steak, comes pride. God hates the proud. God opposes the proud (see Proverbs 8:13, among others). Take note: as a leader, you do not want to be in a position where God chooses to oppose you. That does not seem workable at all. God is a dreadful enemy.

Jesus shares the antidote. This first leadership principle, so counterintuitive, comes straight from the mouth of Jesus. You want to be great? First, you must become a servant. The most overused phrase in our overhyped society may be "this changes everything." But Jesus's view on leadership truly changed everything. Jesus came to serve and he came to lead—both/and. Leaders serve those they lead. Jesus taught that leaders become a "slave" to those who follow. Could Jesus possibly have used stronger language? To be first, you have to go to the back of the line. A leader does not eat until everyone else has filled their plates, even if that means scraping the pans. Then a leader washes the dishes. Serving—that's what leadership is about.

Jesus demonstrated this principle in John 13, when he washed the disciples' feet, a humble role normally reserved for servants or slaves. Jesus showed that he could clean the dirt from between toes and in so doing laid out a blueprint for future leaders to follow. Jesus is the master and if Jesus can wash feet, then you'd better believe that you and I should learn to wash and dry them as well. You are not a leader if you are too proud to take out the trash or too busy to pay attention to a person interrupting your workflow. You cannot lead without serving. That's what Jesus taught and that's what Jesus lived. Now, go and do likewise.

CHAPTER TWENTY-THREE

THE WIDOW

LUKE 21:1-4
MARK 12:41-44

Shuffling up to the contribution box attracted no one's notice. The priests busied themselves with their work and with the better-dressed members of the temple. Lots of older women, many of them widows, moved in and out of the temple during the day. This one in particular fretted about her money but felt compelled to give something back to the Lord. Despite her current status in society, so much good infused her life that she sensed the Lord's graciousness all around her. Even today, she had heard a new rabbi teaching about the Lord's concern for widows. His words seemed intended especially for her. The Lord notices widows and orphans, even if the religious leaders busy themselves elsewhere. With a grateful heart, she dropped two small coins—literally all the money she possessed—into the box. No worries, the Lord provides. Moving back through the crowds, she left to discover that provision for the day.

One afternoon Jesus was with his disciples, teaching in the temple in Jerusalem. He had just finished excoriating the religious teachers of day, denouncing them as men who love to both "devour widow's houses" and show off with long, pretentious prayers. Let all of us who spend time talking about God and how to live a life pleasing to him note that Jesus used his most damning language against religious hypocrites. This teaching emphasis should never be far from our minds and hearts.

Just as Jesus ended his sentence about widow's houses and those who would devour them, he looked up and what did he see? A widow making a contribution. Jesus could see that she was poor and Jesus could see what she gave. The widow dropped two small copper coins in the offering box. Older English versions of the Bible call a coin like this a "mite." These were the smallest and least valuable coins in circulation in Judea at that time. It's hard to know the value of these coins relative to today's monetary system, but suffice it to say that at the most, it wouldn't add up to more than a buck. More shocking than the amount is the fact that Jesus knew that these paltry coins are all the money the widow had to live on. Because he's Jesus, he could both recognize her financial situation and look into her heart. She had just given all she had. The rich people around her, while giving much greater sums of cash, in no way matched her sacrifice.

I recently watched a television program about a group of billionaires who have pledged to give at least one half of their fortunes away to charity before they die. Without question a worthy goal. Many good causes will benefit and untold lives around the world will be influenced in positive ways. In no way would I ever want to communicate that these gifts are not admirable. This is a good example of how we should give and how we usually give—out of our abundance. If you have been given a great deal, then the right thing to do is to share it with others less fortunate. *I have plenty—here, have some of mine.*

Nonetheless, Jesus did not applaud that sort of giving. Jesus dismissed it, in a sense, and instead pointed to the widow, who gave all she had to live on, her last dollar. The widow gave sacrificially; she gave, knowing it would hurt. The widow gave, understanding that she may not eat; she gave even though she was impoverished. To my mind, the widow gave *foolishly*. Yet Jesus praised this manner of giving.

Generosity. That's the lesson for leaders. Where do you and I need to give? Where do we give politely when we need to give sacrificially? Or even foolishly? This involves our money as Jesus so powerfully points out to us. But giving like this can also apply to our time and our energy and our expertise and our influence. Where do we need to go from being an occasional giver to being a lavish giver? By this I mean a person who is unrestrained, practicing a generosity that you will feel in the morning. What would it take for you to become a truly generous person?

Ponder this idea for a minute—if you were a multi-billion-aire, where would you spend your money? Would you buy yachts or mansions or islands? Personally, I would buy the St. Louis Cardinals and give everyone in the stands a free slice of pizza every time a Cardinal hit a home run. How about you? Could you give away half of your fortune? Or maybe up to ninety-nine percent? Let's face it, most of us won't get the chance to control billions of dollars or own our favorite sports franchise. But all of us will be and have been given something. Most of us will be given money and resources far in excess of what other people around the world possess and far more than people throughout history even dreamed of. How will you deal with your wealth? Will you take the risk of living generously? Jesus instructed us to look to the widow. The widow gave it all. Deliberate on this aggressive teaching, maybe the most challenging words of Jesus to our affluent ears today. Give sacrificially. Give in a way that costs you something. As a leader, think often of the widow as you think of living generously.

CHAPTER TWENTY-FOUR

NICODEMUS

JOHN 3, 7-12, 19

Nicodemus had heard the talk going around about a rabbi—this one was different, and there were crowds who clamored to hear him in Jerusalem. While intriguing to hear from someone new, Nicodemus felt like something more, something greater might be in play. Could this actually be the one promised in the Scriptures, the long-awaited Messiah? Nicodemus felt a tug to go see Jesus in person. But Nicodemus also knew the scorn of the religious leaders toward Jesus. So, better to dialogue with Jesus in a private setting, away from the judgmental eyes of his fellow Pharisees and avoid their condemnation. Nicodemus wasn't ready to make waves. Safer to approach Jesus in the dark.

Nicodemus was a Pharisee and a ruler of the Jews, a learned man, a scholar, highly religious and committed to his Jewish faith. Nicodemus showed a trait that good scholars (and leaders) tend to possess – curiosity. However, he was also a careful person, so Nicodemus chose to visit Jesus at night, after the light long faded from the sky. He wanted a conversation with this fascinating yet disconcerting teacher who turned heads everywhere, but he didn't want anyone to know about it. Nicodemus was not prepared to sacrifice his reputation for a renegade teacher named Jesus. This was understandable. There's a lot on the line for Nicodemus and he'd never even met Jesus.

Nicodemus's first words of greeting reveal a bit of what he's been thinking about Jesus. "Rabbi, we know you are a teacher come from God, for no one can do these signs you do unless God is with him." It's pretty doubtful that Nicodemus said these words to anyone else his entire life. Something about Jesus shook him to his core. If you're a leader and a Christian, then Jesus should shake you to your core. Like Nicodemus, Jesus should exhibit a pull on your life that you can't really explain. Jesus is compelling, fascinating, intimidating, frightening, and comforting. Never blasé. If that's the case then you don't know Jesus and you should reread the Gospel of John several times this week. Jesus should never be far from the center of your mind. Nicodemus had not decided what he ultimately thought about Jesus, but he had decided that he needed to know more. Jesus might be a lot of different things to a lot of different people, but Jesus cannot be boring. If so, then you haven't thought enough about Jesus—and Nicodemus had been thinking.

I like proof. I tend to ask questions and wonder why a lot. I'm not likely to buy in until I see some evidence. However, I'm also curious and am drawn to ideas beyond my knowing. Having a degree in biology, I've been trained in the methodologies of science—but I also have this suspicion that all we see is not all there is. I think many of us feel this way and this is one reason I'm drawn to the story of Nicodemus. I would have been more comfortable approaching Jesus quietly, away from prying eyes and contrary opinions. I would have carefully guarded my reputation. I too would have gone to Jesus in the dark.

The words Jesus spoke to Nicodemus are some of the best known in all Scripture, even in all of religious teaching. Jesus told Nicodemus, "Unless one is born again he cannot see the kingdom of God." A few minutes later in their conversation, Jesus made the way to eternal life clear to Nicodemus and to all humanity when he said, "For God loved the world so much that he gave his only Son, that whoever believes in him should not perish but have eternal life." Jesus brought clarity to Nicodemus's questions. In doing so, Jesus drew a contrast between light and darkness. "Whoever does what is true comes to the light," Jesus told Nicodemus. Of course, both men knew no sun shone in the sky during this discussion. Darkness settled in and stayed in the ancient world. Nicodemus understood the metaphor, the meaning behind it and the decision that followed. Jesus, the masterful teacher, left Nicodemus with a lot to think about, and Nicodemus was a thinker.

After this initial interaction with Jesus on that dark night, we don't hear much about Nicodemus. During an argument among the Pharisees he offered a timid defense of Jesus (John 7:50), but was rebuffed and so backed off. As the final events of Jesus's life on earth unfolded, Nicodemus remained in the background, a passive observer, deciding whether the comfort of the shadows offered more safety than the alternative of following Jesus. They did. They still do.

Nicodemus would not have been uninformed, however. In his role as a leader of the Jews he would have sat in the vortex of the news about Jesus. Nicodemus heard Jesus claim to be "the light of the world." With his fellow Pharisees he met the blind man whom Jesus healed, thus bringing light into this man's darkness. How the words and works of Jesus must have rung in his head at night, being a thinking man, one who lay awake and pondered these events. Nicodemus wrestled with his anxieties. Even as he grew more convinced of the truth about Jesus, he feared the wrath of his peers among the ruling class. Nicodemus watched the trial and arrest and crucifixion of Jesus in silence. How did he feel? Shocked? Saddened? Disgusted at himself for not doing more to save an innocent man? Those were dark days for Nicodemus.

As a leader, you will face dark days. As a leader, you will sometimes fail to stand your ground when you should. As a leader, you will fold sometimes and hurt others in the process. That's part of leading. You will have regrets, as anyone who has truly led others through difficult endeavors will attest—but it's never too late to do the right thing. It is never too late for a leader to step into the light. After the crucifixion, Nicodemus experienced his own rebirth, right before the resurrection of Jesus. Nicodemus stepped from darkness into light.

We witness this new Nicodemus, one no longer ruled by his fears and what others think about him, in John 19:38-42. He stepped from the back of the crowd, helped take the body of Jesus off of the cross and lay it in a tomb. This was no small gesture, and one which proved to be costly in a lot of ways—financially, politically, and socially. Nicodemus no longer questioned in the shadows, but fully embraced Jesus and strode into the light. Amazingly, Nicodemus did not even need the resurrection to understand the goodness and hope found in Jesus. He had been thinking about

Jesus for months and months. Nicodemus sacrificed his reputation to bury Jesus because it was the right thing to do and Nicodemus had grown weary of not doing the right thing. Imagine his joy a couple of days later when he heard that the body he so carefully helped prepare for burial had disappeared. Jesus was alive! Of the many joyous people hearing that news, his delight had to be among the greatest. Nicodemus fully committed himself on the day Jesus died, disregarding the cost. Think of the confirmation the resurrection brought him. A leader steps into the light regardless of the price tag.

Nicodemus asked questions. It's not unusual for a leader to doubt and question. That's a sign of an active mind and a spirit coming to grips with reality. Doubts and questions help us to develop our beliefs; our beliefs harden into convictions and convictions guide our actions. Without wrestling with our doubts, we fail to mature into a deep leader. Struggling with issues and misgivings helps a leader grow into a person who rejects the appeal of praise and the inertia of passivity. Questioning helps a leader step into the light with confidence and faith, striding out as a devoted follower of Jesus. Our journey as disciples of Christ proves long and eventful. Jesus urges us toward the light when we might find more attraction in the anonymity of the shade. Take heart in our friend Nicodemus. Legend describes Nicodemus as an open follower of Jesus in the years following the resurrection, living in Jerusalem and arguing with anyone who would listen about the reality of the risen Christ.

Nicodemus traveled a lot like you and I do as we take our voyage of faith. He first found Jesus interesting. Nicodemus checked out the gossip at the source, but put off making a decision about Jesus. He later faced ridicule during his journey and almost let fear and doubt and the opinions of others completely turn him away from Jesus. Finally, something clicked. While for their first meeting years before, Nicodemus had walked up to Jesus in the dark of night, for their final one he approached the broken body of Jesus in the full light of day. Nicodemus moved to the cross with conviction, shouldering through the ranks of his former colleagues in order to do so, fully aware of what this act would cost him. Nicodemus chose to walk in the light. Shall we join him?

CHAPTER TWENTY-FIVE

ACTS 9

The message was clear. Unambiguous. No doubt from the Lord, the significance of it rocked Ananias, leaving him confused and frightened. He was to present himself to the chief prosecutor of the fledgling Christian faith. A man to hide your babies from rather than to embrace, a man to avoid at all costs. Saul—brilliant and murderous—tormented Christians, yet the Lord sent Ananias to actually help him in his time of pain and confusion. Ananias meeting with Saul represents the bravery of many, many Christians who followed him over the centuries.

Saul, an energetic zealot, saw Christians not as people but as problems. His life work morphed into the eradication of this new dangerous sect of Judaism. Not only did he approve of the murder of Stephen, the first martyr of the early church, but he set out to add to the list of beaten and imprisoned followers of Jesus. Today we might call him a radicalized fanatic, even a terrorist. Saul certainly spread terror as he pursued anyone who lined his or her life up with

Jesus. *This* was the Saul who Ananias had heard of when the Lord sent him on this mission. Ananias did not know of Saul's dramatic encounter with the risen Christ on the road to Damascus. Ananias did not know of Saul's remarkable change of heart, or his new devotion to Jesus, or of his humble conversion. The Lord didn't fill in many details as he sent Ananias to Saul's aid.

Ananias questioned the Lord and received scant details in return. The Lord had plans for Saul, plans involving both speaking before kings and plans for suffering and humility. Ananias left immediately. No pause is recorded, no taking a night to sleep on it or time to kiss his family goodbye, maybe for the last time. Ananias walked to Saul's house, placed his hands on Saul and prayed. Ananias even welcomed Saul to his new club of Christ-followers by calling him "brother." From despised enemy to brother. Only then did the scales fall from Saul's eyes.

Leading involves bravery. Ananias showed us the way by going to meet Saul. Ananias walked straight into the house of a man who could kill him and his family. That's bravery. Some might say foolhardy, but it paints for us a picture of faith. Ananias heard God speak, so he went. Acting on faith always involves a level of bravery. Even if you go with questions in mind, just like Ananias, you demonstrate bravery when you step out your door. You don't just think bravely, you act bravely. You may feel brave in your mind, but unless you follow up that thought with action, you're only daydreaming. The world holds lots of daydreamers, far fewer brave leaders.

Saul, soon to change his name to Paul, demonstrated bravery throughout his life as he spread the gospel across the Roman world. Whether in beatings, shipwrecks, persecutions, or facing crowds filled with hateful people just like he once was, Paul stood bravely for the Lord. There is no more powerful example of bravery in Scripture except for Jesus himself—and maybe Ananias, the quiet man just living out his faith, who quickly and unreservedly acted on the Lord's command. Ananias left home that day to heal the devil himself. God used his hands to remove the scales from Saul's eyes and from Paul's heart. In doing so, God used Ananias to change a life that changed the world. A simple man acted in brave obedience. This happens every day. May God grant us the grace to do the same.

CHAPTER TWENTY-SIX

ACTS 12

An elderly gentleman arrived at the hospital I was working at one summer, complaining about a lack of feeling in his feet, unaware that he suffered from the effects of untreated diabetes. I helped patients in the emergency room get settled, taking their health history and preparing them to see the nurses and physicians. This was a summer job, one I sought due to my interest in the field of medicine. While I had already seen a great deal that summer, as a newcomer to the medical world, I was totally unprepared for what we found when this man removed his shoes and socks.

Because of poor circulation in his feet, ulcers had developed, which he could not feel due to numbness accompanying his diabetes. The open sores festered and became infected, the flesh literally dying on the tops of his feet. The injury did not surprise me so much. However, the maggots wriggling in the flesh on both of his feet turned my stomach. While trying to remain as professional as a college student wading into uncharted physical maladies could do, I helped pick the maggots off this man's feet, who remained friendly and positive throughout. Needless to say, my summer experience trumped those of my friends who worked at the pool. In reality, the maggots likely saved this man's feet. By eating the dead flesh, they helped contain the growing infection and staved off potential amputation. Maggots had been used in this way therapeutically over the centuries. I've never forgotten the first sight of those wriggling larva when his socks came off.

Herod Antipas also had issues with worms. Herod was a nasty ruler. He arrested and persecuted members of the newly developing Christian faith. He threw Peter in prison and had James, the brother of John, put to death by the sword. More than anything, Herod loved himself. After one speech, the crowds, no doubt spurred on by fear of their malicious king, shouted that his voice was like that of the gods. Herod arrogantly drank it all in. But the Lord decided enough was enough. Herod met a particularly grisly end. Struck down by an angel and eaten by worms, Herod departed this life like no one else. At least he was unique in death. One modern researcher believes Herod succumbed to chronic kidney disease complicated by a case of maggot-infested gangrene of the testicles.

The book of Acts makes it clear that Herod ultimately died of *pride*, of putting himself in the place of God and of forgetting who allowed him to serve as a king in the first place. Proverbs 16:5 pronounces, "The Lord detests all the proud of heart. Be sure of this; they will not go unpunished." We fail to grasp just how much our Lord hates pride. Let this image of Herod and his demise drive the point home. God is infinitely creative. Who could imagine sending such a message, of painting us a picture of God's hatred for arrogance, any more than Luke does for us here? Luke, a physician and the author of Acts, took special notice of this case. A leader watches his heart. A leader prays for humility and asks the Lord to root out pride. Let the maggots in Herod's undershorts serve as a warning for us all – God seriously opposes pride and arrogance.

 PRISCILLA & AQUILA

ACTS 18

The employment market for tentmakers collapsed about 1,000 years ago. Of course, outside of the overrated practice of camping, no one lives in tents for any length of time, except for some Bedouins grazing their flocks in the Middle East. Not much call for skilled tentmakers in this era. But back in the first century, tentmaking was a good gig. Priscilla and Aquila, living in Corinth, sewed tents and hosted the Apostle Paul during his stay in their city. Paul was also trained in the art of tentmaking—and so we meet the most remembered trio of tentmakers in history.

Priscilla and Aquila, not native Corinthians, settled there after being booted out of Rome by the Emperor Claudius as part of an expulsion of Jews from the city. Like Paul, Priscilla and Aquila were Jews who had embraced the Messiah. Also like Paul, they answered the missionary call to the world. They traveled with Paul on one of his missionary journeys around the Mediterranean and stayed for a time in Ephesus. While there, Priscilla and Aquila sat under the teaching of a dynamic young preacher, Apollos of Alexandria. Apollos spoke with eloquence and knowledge of the available scriptures, but he was not fully versed in the teachings of Jesus. Into his life stepped Priscilla and Aquila, who instructed him more accurately while he continued to share the good news about Jesus around the region.

What makes this couple of tentmakers, briefly mentioned in the New Testament, so impressive for leaders? Perhaps we might overlook this point today, but Priscilla was a woman in a prominent leadership role in the early church. Her husband, Aquila, is never mentioned without his wife. Six times, their names surface in various accounts in the New Testament and always their names appear side-by-side. Three times Aquila's name comes first and three times Priscilla is mentioned first. They were a dynamic duo. Paul trusted them, traveled with them, lived with them, and befriended them. You build a good team with people you like to spend time with, not just in ministry, but also in the everyday things of life, like fixing dinner and mending tents. Paul never relegates Priscilla to a second-tier status. Priscilla's part in the developing religion both sent a strong message about the place of women in Christianity and pushed against the culture of the day. Women and men around them noticed. Priscilla did not need to hold back or mask her leadership gifts because she was a woman. She led well as her husband, Aquila, and her friend, Paul, encouraged her role in the church.

Another aspect of leadership we notice with Priscilla and Aquila involves their chosen profession of tent making. Leaders show up from all places. Everyone is just a kid from somewhere. Jesus chose fishermen as disciples and Paul chose tentmakers as missionaries. Their profession helped them pay their bills and open doors in new cities, like Corinth. God will use whatever skills you possess and whatever background you hail from as you step out and lead. Don't overlook the parts of your life that don't seem particularly "spiritual." All sorts of doors open to all sorts of keys. Who can say what aspects of leadership the keys of your past will unlock?

"Generous" describes Priscilla and Aquila. They were giving people. They helped Paul in Corinth, traveled with him to Ephesus and took the time to instruct Apollos. Generosity is a powerful trait of good leaders. Priscilla and Aquila, generous with their time, money, reputation and advice, asked for nothing in return. A mountain of good happens when generous leaders branch out. Generosity fosters goodwill and creates an inclination to listen. People follow a generous leader.

Finally, overlooked is the fact that Priscilla and Aquila were some of the first leaders in the early church who never had a direct encounter with Jesus. Most of the original disciples were still alive at this time and Paul encountered Jesus in a miraculous way in the road to Damascus. Priscilla and Aquila represent the next generation and all the generations that follow, down to us today. They led as disciples of Jesus, based not on their eyes but on their hearts. Never having personally interacted with Jesus, they still became devoted followers of him, some of the first as the faith spread across the Roman Empire. It is challenging to be among the first of a movement, but that's where you find leaders. Beyond the apostles and beyond Paul, the Christian movement rooted and began to grow. Priscilla and Aquila represent that early growth and embody the passing of a crucial test for the faith. Because of Priscilla and Aquila and similar leaders, the sacred teachings of Jesus came down to us today. Now, billions of people share those blessings. Priscilla and Aquila invested their lives for the early churches and for that Paul commended them (Romans 16:4). Now we join Paul in commending them in our generation.

PAUL AND HIS POSSE

COLOSSIANS 4

Think, for a moment, of Paul's life. In and out of jail. Beaten by the authorities. Whipped. Stoned. Adrift at sea. Shipwrecked. Standing on the banks of raging rivers hell-bent to cross. Confronting robbers. Dodging enemies. Hungry, thirsty, sleepless, cold, exposed. Resolute. Restive. Ever on the road. Dictating letters to his protégés. Worrying persistently about the status of the various churches he started. Carrying the weight of the expanding Jesus movement upon his shoulders. Yet never going it alone.

Paul traveled far and wide. He was a late convert to the Christian faith, a learned man and the greatest missionary the church has ever seen. Paul took the good news of Jesus all around the Roman world, as far west as Spain and to the major cities of the empire, including Athens and Rome. We speak highly of his life and influence on the Christian faith. After Jesus, no one did more to develop and spread Christianity. But Paul was never alone. He never worked or traveled alone. Paul always surrounded himself with worthy companions, whom he mentions often at the end of his letters recorded in the New Testament.

We find one such list of colleagues in the closing section of Paul's letter to the church at Colossae, an ancient city in Asia Minor. This letter of instruction to the church was to be read aloud to the congregation, then passed around and discussed so that all the church members could understand Paul's teaching. It is a superb dispatch relating to the believers in Colossae—and to us today—on how we can walk closely with Jesus and live a life filled with his grace and power. In Paul's closing comments we gain insight into his ministry companions—Paul's posse, if you will. The final paragraphs speak to us about some remarkable people who are easily passed over in our study of the Bible.

Tychicus (pronounced "tick-a-kus") visited this young church in Colossae personally at Paul's request. Paul uses the word "faithful" to describe Tychicus, and with good reason. This is not the only place where Paul mentions Tychicus, who served as Paul's mailman, carrying Paul's letters to various churches in the Mediterranean world. Not only was there no email, there was no regular postal service in those days. A trustworthy person was needed to carry these priceless letters to their intended audiences. Someone faithful. Tychicus was that man. A little Bible sleuthing and it appears that Tychicus carried the letters that later became the books of Colossians, Ephesians, Philemon and Titus in the New Testament. What if Tychicus slacked off? No way. He was one of Paul's most trusted team members. Paul and the newly developing churches could count on Tychicus. You and I enjoy the fruit of his faithfulness every time we open our Bibles. Good leaders are faithful even in anonymity and good leaders follow-through on tasks handed to them.

Following Tychicus, Paul mentions Onesimus, a former slave who Paul met in Rome and guided to Christ. Then appears Aristarchus, Paul's fellow prisoner, who was arrested alongside him during a riot in Ephesus (Acts 19:29) and who also traveled with Paul to Rome. As a tough, battle-hardened follower of Jesus, Aristarchus earned Paul's trust. You raised your game if you ran with Paul.

Then comes Mark, the writer of the gospel that bears his name. Mark must have been faithful, right? Well, not always. Paul split with an earlier companion, Barnabas, over the character of this very same Mark. It seems that Mark had quit the company a few years before (Acts 15:36-40) but later returned. At the outset of the next journey, Paul, in no mood to gamble a spot on his team to a deserter, planned to leave Mark behind. Barnabas, however, saw something worthy in this undeveloped young man and wished to give him a second chance. Paul and Barnabas argued, disagreed sharply and split company over Mark. Divisions occur even when godly people do ministry together. Mark's early reputation was that of one who bailed when circumstances got tough (see Mark 14:51, which is thought to be an autobiographical reference to Mark. Look it up—the man ran naked through the streets of Jerusalem). But as Paul wrote this letter years later, Mark stood at his side. What changed? Mark did. Mark matured and proved Barnabas right. Mark developed into a faithful follower of Jesus and neither Mark nor Paul held a grudge from their earlier encounters. In fact, at the very end of his life, in some of his last words before his death, Paul wrote that he needed Mark with him (2 Timothy 4:11). That is a powerful word about a trusted friend. Remember this lesson: Good leaders give people a second chance. Developing into a proven leader involves taking hits and experiencing failures. Like we see with Mark, a second chance may pay off big. Don't deny that to others or yourself.

Paul commended several other members of his company. One was Jesus Justus, who was a great comfort to Paul while he was in prison (and whose name would be fabulous for a rock band). Then we meet Epaphras, the founder of the church at Colossae and one who fervently prayed for the church. Luke, a physician and the author of both the Acts of the Apostles and the Gospel of Luke, traveled often with his close friend Paul. The recognition of Nympha, a woman and a leader in the early church, reveals the valued role women played in the spread of the Christian faith and the respect Paul had for this friend.

A chilling reference follows as the roll call moves forward, a warning for disciples throughout the centuries, a remark about Demas. At the time of this writing, Demas was working with Paul and living the faith. He was one with the others, a valuable part of the team. Later, however, Demas fell in love with the things of the world, deserted Paul and abandoned his missionary friends. Sounds like Mark's story, only with an unfortunate ending. One is never too far along, or too immersed in a strong leadership culture, to tumble away toward the enticements of the world. Pray that you avoid the fate of Demas.

Relationships matter. Relationships shape leaders. The people you spend time with change you. Good leaders put themselves with quality people. Paul knew this truth and lived it. As a leader, place yourself around the table with authentic people, trusted and honest friends and colleagues. Good leaders require good companions. Who's in your posse?

CHAPTER TWENTY-NINE

LOIS

2 TIMOTHY 1

Grandmas are the best. The Bible talks more about grand-mothers that one might think. Remember Joash's evil grandmother, Athaliah? Now, let's meet a grandma from the other end of the spectrum, someone we'd want to spend time with. Lois is famous, revered through the ages, because she was a godly grandmother. Timothy, her grandson, traveled as a missionary with Paul and developed some of the first successful churches. Timothy grew to become one of Paul's closest friends and confidants. Paul was encouraged by his sincere faith and Paul addressed his last known written correspondence (the book of 2 Timothy) to Timothy.

Genuine faith never appears out of thin air. Timothy absorbed it from his mother, Eunice, and his grandmother, Lois. Paul knew them both and perceived their faith as the spring that watered the flowering of Timothy's commitment to the Lord. Neither Timothy's father, who was thought to be Greek, nor Timothy's grandfather, are mentioned in the text. Timothy's faith developed from his matriarchal lineage.

A strong and sincere faith is not guaranteed from one generation to the next. Many well-meaning parents apply all the religious parenting techniques currently in vogue only to see their children reject the faith, or ignore the faith, or quietly set the faith aside. Christianity is only one generation deep. Every generation must believe afresh. Lois did something right. Too bad we don't know her practices as we could use them to develop a series of books, podcasts and video guides on how to raise children of faith. We could dub it the "Lois-ization" of our children. I would have bought it when my kids were little. However, we do own one clue about her methodology—her faith is described as "sincere."

"Sincere" is defined by Webster's dictionary as being "free from pretenses or deceit; not hypocritical, genuine, wholehearted, real, honest, frank, upfront, candid, on the level, pure." Our children sniff out hypocrisy in our lives and our words as parents. When we act one way in front of others and a totally different way at home, the kids notice. They start to surmise that the Christian faith that their parents profess is not fully realized, not efficacious, and not deeply meaningful. They correctly deduce that if that's all there is to the Christian faith, then no need to waste their time here. Plenty of other good things to pursue on a Sunday morning.

What holds for a parent holds for a leader. No effective apologetic exists for hypocrisy. A leader who is fake or pretentious really is not a leader at all, but merely a figurehead, a placeholder. This person might hold the position of boss or director, but he is not a leader others will follow wholeheartedly. You may work for a two-faced supervisor because there's a steady paycheck in it, but you'll bolt when a better opportunity comes along. Hypocrisy manufactures a legacy of disbelief, disengagement and distance. True for parents and true for leaders.

This was not true of Lois. Her sincere faith refreshed Paul and molded Timothy. You are never alone as you live out your faith. Our sincerity does not fade away in vain, even if we do not see the results. Two old sayings come to mind when I think of Lois and the many godly grandmothers who followed in her path. The first reminds us that "the hand that rocks the cradle is the hand that rules the world." Good leadership, like good parenting, imprints qualities on the next generation. If another old saying is true, that "our most important contributions are the ones we leave behind," then the legacy left by Lois will be hard to surpass. Forever stamped in Scripture, this quiet grandmother's endowment offers us much to ponder as parents, grandparents and leaders.

CHAPTER THIRTY

A GREAT CLOUD OF WITNESSES

HEBREWS 11 & 12

Every sport enshrines its heroes in a hall of fame. Baseball, football, basketball, bowling—you can visit them all. This is where the outstanding men and women of each pastime remind us mortals of their greatness. The New Testament contains a hall of fame as well, a roll call of heroes "of whom the world was not worthy." Provocative words spring off the page describing how these saints lived their faith. Flogged, tortured, sawn in two, chopped apart, mistreated and outcast, their stories remind us that godly people lived their faith in constant peril.

We don't know for sure who wrote the book of Hebrews and recorded this list of saints. Some scholars believe that the Apostle Paul authored the book. Other leading candidates include Barnabas, Luke, Apollos and Priscilla. We may never know for sure, but whoever wrote this letter believed in understanding history. The author did not want the readers to forget the sacrifices made for them by their ancestors in the faith.

I have visited the British National Gallery in London on multiple occasions. What a privilege to wander among a stunning art collection compiled from masters over the centuries. A surprising amount of the art focuses on the martyrs of the Christian faith. Dozens of paintings reflect some aspect of this theme. Ironically, all the people portrayed as martyrs in these paintings lived after those mentioned in Hebrews. Over and over, from the time of the Hebrews account to the modern day, men and women suffered and at times died for their faith in Jesus.

Leaders should remember heroes of the faith, whether they know some personally or through the stories found in the Bible. While some heroes won great victories, others simply lived a quiet life and continued faithfully to the end. From Moses to Mother Teresa, heroes surround us. It's encouraging to know of those who've gone before us, to realize that we're one of a long line of Jesus followers.

The author of Hebrews introduces us to an idea that we don't often consider. Apparently we are "surrounded" by a great cloud of witnesses, the men and women who lived and died for their faith. Picture yourself running a marathon, where all along the route people cheer for you and call you by name. In some unknown way, faithful men and women who've gone before us continue to encourage us in our efforts to run with Jesus. Perhaps they stand atop the chariots of fire we read about earlier in this book. We cannot see them and we cannot hear them, but they are near. Who lines the path you're running? Sounds like Caleb, Rahab, Jonathan and Daniel stand shouting. Priscilla, Aquila and Paul await your arrival a few paces over. Many more who've lived for Christ throughout the centuries choose prime spots. Included in the group are your ancestors who followed Jesus. Maybe a godly grandparent looks on expectantly. Perhaps even the early Christians from your tribe, tongue, or nation. Regardless, they stand present. Watching you, willing you on, applauding your steps of faith.

What does a leader do in light of this great cloud of witnesses? A leader remembers. A leader reminds those seeking to follow Jesus that they are not the first. Not the first to follow Jesus. Not the first to face trials and disruptions and pain and ridicule and doubts and opposition. Not the first to fail and gloriously, not the first to triumph.

A strong motivation for this book and for mining these stories from the Bible is my desire for you to see and remember. Hopefully, you will better appreciate the enduring qualities of the heroes of the Bible. You'll comprehend how their stories and lessons are timeless, applicable today, and never outdated. Then you can go and help others remember. In a world filled with noise and flashing lights, the Bible brings a solidity not experienced among other teachings and resources. It is real, when other things with which we fill our hearts prove to be false and fleeting.

The author of Hebrews wanted us to remember the heroes of our past and gain encouragement for our present. Someday, we will pass from this life, leaving the race to others as we step into our place among the great cloud of witnesses. Who do you hope to cheer on? If you are my descendant and are reading this as you follow Jesus, know that I am cheering you on. Help others run the race and you'll be there to welcome them as they finish their course. Think of how splendid the long-awaited arrival of those on their victory lap will feel. Like winning the world championship and the lottery and free pizza for life all rolled into one. Simply magnificent. Work towards glory and start influencing your world today. A leader learns from those who've come before. Then, a leader remembers and a leader reminds and a leader steps out into the new arenas of faith found in our present day.

CONCLUSION

"Be strong and courageous." Standing next to his friend Caleb, looking over the lands spread before them, Joshua faced the daunting task of leading an army into enemy territory. Failure meant the destruction of his people. Success felt elusive. On the cusp of his greatest moment as a general and the ultimate victory of his nation, Joshua felt fearful. Although a veteran leader, Joshua still needed to hear these words spoken from the mouth of God. "Be strong and courageous. Do not be afraid; do not be discouraged, for the Lord your God will be with you wherever you go." Braced by this pledge, Joshua crossed the Jordan River into the promised land.

We encounter stories about leaders every day. Brutal leaders cling to power by oppressing their people. Dishonest leaders loot the coffers of their countries or their companies for personal gain. Passive leaders fail to act, and innocents bear the brunt of that dereliction of duty. Leadership matters. Poor decisions by kings and czars and prime ministers led to World War I and the deaths of millions. Following soon after those rulers, a new group of leaders, hardened in the chaos and frustration of that war, launched World War II, hastening the deaths of millions more—the sons and daughters of those who suffered through the first one. Poor leadership brought unnecessary pain, suffering and death to millions the world over.

On the other hand, good leaders bless generations. John R. Mott helped thousands of young people cross the oceans to be the voice and hands of Jesus through the Student

Volunteer Movement, and received the Nobel Peace Prize for his efforts. Winston Churchill provided a steady hand and clarity of focus during Britain's darkest hour. Martin Luther King, Jr., shared vision and hope and courage to people refused their freedoms in a nation with a constitution guaranteeing those very freedoms. Nelson Mandela of South Africa brought peaceful change to a society sitting atop a racial powder keg. Good leaders provided the funds to produce polio vaccines and to eradicate smallpox. Today leaders pave the roads, defend the innocent, feed the hungry, educate young people, and provide clean water. And on and on. Most of the benefits we enjoy in our modern society can be attributed to a benevolent God and good leaders. The challenges faced by our world will only be surmounted by the work of quality men and women as they lead. Good leaders rise to solve problems.

Today's era stands as one of the most challenging in which to lead in spiritually. Pressures abound that turn the heads of those trying to walk in a way that emulates Jesus. Social media blesses and curses, while always hovering within arm's length. Entertainers rise and fall like fireworks, fads swing in and out of our lives. People come and go. We move often and switch jobs regularly. The noise of life barrages us constantly. We hear leaders of various enterprises telling us how to lead, but in a few years those same leaders fade away. What's solid in today's world? Where can we sink foundations that hold? Bedrock is the Bible, the ancient text filled with lessons from past lives. The teachings of Moses and Jesus and Paul and all the biblical authors center us in regard to this world and the world to come. These teachings benefited generations before being handed down to us. Writings that live and breathe and delve into our soul due to the work of the Holy Spirit, now that's unique. Here lies solid ground to stand upon and build a life and a legacy.

Like Joshua, perhaps you stand on the cusp of something epic. Or like the rest of us, likely your challenge is a bit more conventional. Regardless, step forward into the areas of leadership and influence before you. Read again and again the captivating stories of men and women in scripture. As I mentioned in the beginning of this book, make the Bible your primary life text. Let the words found within lead you to encounter God in deeper ways. Experiencing God brings joy and meaning and hope to your life, and thus allows you to bring joy and meaning and hope to others. Finally, always keep in mind the Lord's promise to Joshua, which also happens to be the Lord's promise to you; "Be strong and courageous. Do not be afraid; do not be discouraged, for the Lord your God will be with you wherever you go."

(FROM THE MESSAGE)

The mark of a good leader is loyal followers; leadership is nothing without a following.
Proverbs 14:28

A good leader motivates, doesn't mislead, doesn't exploit.
Proverbs 16:10

Good leaders abhor wrongdoing of all kinds; sound leadership has a moral foundation.
Proverbs 16:12

Good leaders cultivate honest speech; they love advisors who tell them the truth.
Proverbs 16:13

An intemperate leader wreaks havoc in lives; you're smart to stay clear of someone like that.
Proverbs 16:14

Good tempered leaders invigorate lives; they're like spring rain and sunshine.
Proverbs 16:15

Quick tempered leaders are like mad dogs—cross them and they bite your head off.
Proverbs 20:2

Leaders who know their business and care keep a sharp eye out for the shoddy and cheap, For who among us can be trusted to be always diligent and honest?
Proverbs 20:8-9

After careful scrutiny, a wise leader makes a clean sweep of rebels and dolts.
Proverbs 20:26

Love and truth form a good leader; sound leadership is founded on loving integrity.
Proverbs 20:28

Good leadership is a channel of water controlled by God; he directs it to whatever ends he chooses.
Proverbs 21:1

God loves the pure-hearted and well-spoken; good leaders also delight in their friendship.
Proverbs 22:11

Among leaders who lack insight, abuse abounds, but for one who hates corruption, the future is bright.
Proverbs 28:16

A leader of good judgment gives stability; an exploiting leader leaves a trail of waste.
Proverbs 29:4

When a leader listens to malicious gossip, all the workers get infected with evil.
Proverbs 29:12

Leadership gains authority and respect when the voiceless poor are treated fairly.
Proverbs 29:14

Everyone tries to get help from the leader, but only God will give us justice.
Proverbs 29:26

Leaders can't afford to make fools of themselves, gulping wine and swilling beer, lest, hung over, they don't know right from wrong, and the people who depend on them are hurt.
Proverbs 31:4-5

I want to thank a few people for helping me along the way in writing this book. First, my wife, Dawn, for listening to these stories and encouraging me in the work of putting my thoughts on paper. Second, to the late Howard Hendricks, former professor at Dallas Theological Seminary, for exhorting a group of new staff members with Cru to read the Bible cover to cover, again and again. I took that advice to heart. I know Dr. Hendricks stands among our great cloud of witnesses. Also, to those who helped with editing and insight, especially Patreeya Prasertvit for her thoughtful perspective on writing. Thank you to the team at Cru Press for working this project through to completion with me. Thank you to Jay Lorenzen for introducing me to the twin concepts of care and courage found in great leaders. Finally, thank you to the many wonderful Cru staff and students I've had the privilege of leading, and being led by, over the years. Thank you for your patience with me and your understanding of my failings. Thank you for the lessons you taught me as we shared life and ministry together around the world.

Dave Dishman
Erie, Colorado, 2019